I AM
MY BROTHER'S
KEEPER

Leonard Senft

Produced by:

FriesenPress

Suite 300 – 852 Fort Street
Victoria, BC, Canada V8W 1H8

www.friesenpress.com

Distributed to the trade by The Ingram Book Company

DEDICATION

This book is dedicated to my late mother and
father; a man and woman of FAITH.

CONQUERING GIANTS AND BUILDING LIVES

LEONARD SENFT—a man of faith, a man of insight, and a man of integrity. I was first made aware that there had to be a Mr. Senft when I met his oldest son, Vern, at Bible school some forty-five years ago. Vern was a quiet student, yet diligent and very likeable. I first recall meeting his dad some twenty-four plus years ago when he came to visit his daughter, Sharon, and her husband, Glenn, who were very active in the ministry of Rutland Gospel Tabernacle, where I had just started to pastor.

In 1997, Len and his wife, Rosie, moved to Kelowna and started fellowshipping with us at the church. Len is a man of many talents and abilities but in all that he does, God gets the glory. He is not only the most faithful man at the church, which continued when Rosie was taken into care a number of years ago, but we would often be refreshed with the fruit of his labour—fresh cinnamon rolls and a variety of other goodies that made the tedious tasks of the ministry so much more pleasant. He was also a great student of the Word. He shared a series of teachings on The Journeys of Paul that made the Word come alive.

Len was never afraid to tackle anything that needed doing, whether in ministry, work, or business, if he thought that he could do it. He was a credentialed minister with the Pentecostal Assemblies of Canada and for many years helped to minister and build the church in Rock Creek, both structurally and spiritually. He ministered in most of the small communities in the Boundary Country where he preached, taught, or pastored, filling any vacancy that he found or was called upon to fill. Len had no idea of what the words "quit" and "give up" meant. When it came to standing up for or representing his Lord, no matter what the circumstance or opposition, as the song goes, *he wouldn't bend, he wouldn't bow, he wouldn't burn.*

He has a tremendous ability to identify with people, no matter their background, which created many opportunities for him to share his faith, leading many from every age group—from children at camp or in Sunday school to the aged on their death beds—to a saving knowledge of Jesus Christ. He rarely missed an opportunity to share his testimony of the transforming work and power of Jesus Christ in his life.

His testimony is diverse and powerful: being raised from the dead, killing the giant of alcohol addiction, the varied business endeavours, ministry adventures, and challenges that he faced. All the while, he and Rosie were raising four children of their own and later, fostering two sisters. He was active in civic and community business as well as pastoral and missionary work. His life is a living miracle of God's continued grace, mercy, and intervention.

Reading Len's story may cause acute physical exhaustion because of the amount of activity, work, and ministry described. Do not try this without a prescription from the Great Physician Himself. If it is too much, take a little milk of the Word with it but don't stop until you've taken the complete dose.

Rev. Edward G. "Ted" Bonk.

INTRODUCTION

ON APRIL 15, 2013 I celebrated my eighty-seventh birthday. I now spend more time looking backwards than I do looking forwards. It is this looking backwards that has driven me to write this book. How does one come to terms with his life and how it was lived when he reaches my age?

Hopefully you can say with me that it was lived well and was worthwhile. Two years before I was born, my father promised God that if He gave him a son, he would dedicate him to be a minister of the gospel. The journey my life took from the day I was born until today can only be seen as having the hand of God upon it.

The journey, which almost ended before it began, with a poisoning at the age of two, is just one of the many adventures you will read about. Each adventure I recall proves that God was watching over me, protecting me, and helping me to become the minister that I was destined to be. It wasn't always easy. Many hardships, health issues, and occasionally facing death would all try to hinder the work that God had begun, but God is faithful.

My desire, as you read my story, is that you will see how God's hand on a life starts at birth and continues throughout that life. God loves each and every one. There is never a moment that He is not with you. Whatever path you may find yourself on, God is directing your steps, ever drawing you closer to Him. Each of us has a story and a purpose. I hope that my story will inspire you to believe in God, who created you to live your life to the fullest. With God, each day is truly an adventure.

The telling of my story has been on my mind for several years, but I just couldn't seem to get it started until this year, 2013, when I sat down with paper and pen and started to write. Many times, the stories came to me so fast my hand could not write as quickly as my mind was going. It wasn't many months until my book was finished. With the stories once again vivid in my mind and on paper, I am ever thankful and grateful to my God for leading and directing my life.

In putting this book together, I would like to thank Melody O'Neill, who tirelessly worked through the editing process, and her daughter, Erin O'Neill, for typing it up. I would also like to thank my son-in-law, Glenn Phillips, for designing the front cover, and his wife, (my daughter Sharon) for organizing and getting this book ready for publication.

"I will never leave you nor forsake you." Hebrews 13:5

CHAPTER 1

IN THE BEGINNING

I was always a *wheeler-dealer*—they should have called me *Jacob*, the Bible patriarch who gained a birthright for a mess of pottage. But then you had to be, growing up in the Great Depression, called the Dirty Thirties. Pulling up stakes and moving on was a way of life back then. We tried to eke out a living from the parched earth of the Canadian Prairies, while the merciless, unrelenting winds blew away the topsoil, and a man's dreams. But I wasn't about to let that stop me, and I never missed an opportunity to better myself and get ahead.

It wasn't easy. We were dirt poor—trading goods provided the barest necessities of life, and kept body and soul together. I had a knack for finding deals and spotting a good bargain. But you might say it was my father who made the ultimate bargain—*a bargain with God*. I learned at an early age about the vow he made to the Lord: "You give me a son, and I promise to dedicate him to you to become a minister to preach the Gospel." With such a lofty and noble commitment, you might think the years of my youth were spent living for the Lord and serving Him—*only what's done for Christ will last*. But sad to say, it didn't quite go that way—and I lost my way.

Thirty-five years were to pass before I found my way back. The road I travelled took me on many adventures, until my strength wore out, like a candle burning at both ends. One night, I woke up in the middle of the night with the feeling that someone was hitting me in the chest with a sledgehammer. It was like breathing liquid fire. That was my first heart attack. I was thirty-five years old, had no medication and no doctor. It was only by the grace of God that I didn't die. What I didn't realize that night was that the greatest adventure of my life was just ahead of me. My old life was about to end as I finally surrendered my life to God. But first—I had to do it my way.

My adventure on this earth began April 15, 1926; the night I was born. On my father's side, my family's roots go back to Russia. My grandfather came from Russia. When he and my grandmother emigrated to Canada, he was married and had two small daughters. In Canada, they had eight more children. Their fourth child was a son they named George. He was born on February 8, 1898. George would later become my father.

In those days, education was not compulsory. My grandfather thought that since the boys would be farmers, an education was not necessary. So, consequently, my grandfather did not send my father to school. My father lived until he was eighty-nine years old, without ever learning how to write. However, he taught himself how to read by studying the Bible.

My father married a sixteen-year-old girl, named Bertha Flaig, on December 27, 1921. Soon afterward, they had two daughters, Lenore and Irene.

At the turn of the twentieth century, a great revival was sweeping across many countries of the world. It started in the United States, and eventually came to Canada. In 1925, the revival was happening in southern Saskatchewan. It was here that my father and mother were exposed to it. They accepted the Lord Jesus Christ into their hearts, asking Him to forgive their sins. Born into the family of God and filled with the Holy Spirit, they now had a glorious hope. The day they would say their last goodbyes to this world would be the day they would say their hellos in Heaven – there to live eternally with the Lord.

Camp Revival Meeting in Morse, Saskatchewan in 1924
where my father, George Senft, made a promise to
God to dedicate his son to preach the Gospel.

My father, overjoyed by what he had experienced, could not contain his enthusiasm. He wanted his family, friends, and neighbours to all share in his joy. However, his lack of education and inability to speak English properly made him feel too insecure to be a preacher himself. This is when he decided to make his bargain with God instead, promising God, "If you give me a son, I will dedicate him to You to preach the Gospel."

On April 15, 1926, that son was born. My mother gave birth to me sixteen months after my sister, their second daughter, Irene, was born. After my birth, my mother had a serious nervous breakdown, nearly dying. God, in His mercy, graciously restored her to health. Soon after, two more daughters, Violet and Beatrice, and another son, Ken (born sixteen years later), were added to the family.

Now, eighty-six years later, I want to share the events of my life, which prove that the son who was bargained for and promised to preach the Gospel has fulfilled, and is still fulfilling, that promise.

I Am My Brother's Keeper

CHAPTER 2

MOVING NORTH

While I knew that I had been promised to preach the Gospel, no one had made me aware that I would have an enemy, the devil, who would hinder me at every turn. I was poisoned three times, had three heart attacks, a stroke, and numerous accidents but the devil is no match for the saving and keeping powers of the Lord Jesus Christ.

In 1929, the New York stock exchange collapsed, wiping out many people's life savings. We entered a ten-year depression, the "Dirty Thirties," which was also fittingly called the "Hungry Thirties," because the people were starving. To make matters worse, a drought was causing sandstorms strong enough to blow the fertile topsoil of the farms away. The only things that seemed to thrive were the Russian thistles and the potato bugs.

The potatoes were our lives' mainstay. To combat the potato bugs, a poison powder was sprayed onto the potato plants. One day, my father mixed some of this bug poison with water and poured it into a hand sprayer to pump it onto our potato plants. He went into the house for some reason and told us kids not to touch it. I was about two and a half years old at the time, and I just had to taste it. My eldest sister, Lenore, ran into the house to tell my dad what I had done. When he came out to see, he found me stretched out on my back, stiff as a board, with only the whites of my eyes showing. He carried me into the house, laid me on the bed, and knelt down and prayed, "Lord, you can't let him die. I promised him to You, to preach the Gospel." My father said I came out of it, and soon was outside playing that very same day. On that day, his faith in prayer was established; he knew he could rely on God for anything. He lived to be eighty-nine years old and never once wavered in his faith in prayer.

Me, Leonard, at two years old when I ate the potato bug poison

1929 was a hard year. The dry weather brought a plague of grass-hoppers. They were so abundant that when they lifted off to fly, they darkened out the sun. The sandstorms acted like they were trying to blow us off of the face of the earth. There was no way to keep the sand out of the house. After the table was set, the women would cover the food with a towel to keep the sand off it, and you had to reach under the towel to get at the food.

Talking of food reminds me of a comical incident. On Sundays, we would often have chicken noodle soup and fried chicken for dinner. At this time, there were four kids in the family and we would fight over who was going to get the wishbone. One day, I armed myself with a club, and with my sister Violet, went into the chicken barn. That was a bad day for the chickens. Soon, we came out with a chicken and argued all the way to the house about who would get the wishbone. My mother settled our argument by carrying the chicken back to the chicken barn. It was then she discovered half of the chickens were lame or dragging a wing. When she was through with us, the only thing we were wishing was that we had stayed out of the chicken pen. She didn't even stop to realize she might have caused irreparable damage to this young budding preacher.

The devastating sandstorms were a product of poor farming tech-niques, which depleted the soil, leaving only sand. The settlers that emigrated to Canada after World War I (1914 to 1918) had been drawn to the Prairies by the fertile farmland. The buffalo had been slaughtered and the Prairies offered virgin soil. They put the plough to the soil and harvested some bountiful crops for a few short years. However, mil-lions of acres were turned over, without letting the land lie fallow, and exposure to the sun dried out the soil. The winds blew, and did so for ten to twelve years. Two catastrophic events occurred: the destruc-tion of this farmland, Canada's breadbasket, and the crash of the New York Stock Exchange. The result of this "perfect storm" was that many people lost their life-savings and their farms. These were hard times. People were reported to have died with green grass in their stomachs.

Things had to change, and fast. The government's experimental farms taught the farmers how to "strip farm," to help stop the drifting sandstorms. They also planted new drought-resistant grains. The gov-ernment also used incentives to encourage people to move north, out of the dustbowl.

The North Country was sparsely populated when the government started surveying the land. It was surveyed into sections. The size of one section was 640 acres, then that section was divided into quarters; 160 acres each. The quarters were called homesteads, and any male eighteen-years old and over could apply for one quarter section, for a fee of ten dollars. Within three years, you could get the title. It was legally yours if you had lived on your quarter for at least six months every year, you had dug a well, and had cultivated acreage.

To help with the move north, the Canadian Pacific Railway provided freight cars. In 1931, my family took advantage of the government's help, and decided to make the move north to the Meadow Lake area. The biggest migration north happened from 1927 to 1932. People of many nationalities—English, French, Polish, Ukrainian, and Russian—were among the migrants. This would be the start of a new chapter in our lives; from the dry Prairies into the wet bush country, with all its unforeseen hardships.

CHAPTER 3

OUR HOMESTEAD

We set out north in August of 1931 with our relatives, the Zado family. Since we headed north at the tail end of the migration, our homestead was located on the outside edge of the settlement; about twenty-three miles west of Meadow Lake. My father, my Uncle Zado, and his two older sons rode in the freight cars. The freight cars held our cattle and horses, which needed to be fed and watered, plus our farm machinery and household effects.

We hired a farmer in the area, who had bought a new truck, to drive the wives and kids. He wanted to go north to check out the land for himself. He had heard about this land of milk and honey, and was eager to see it and make a purchase like my father and uncle had done earlier. My mother, my aunt, four kids from our family, and six from my aunt's filled the truck. The farmer also brought his wife and older son, who would help with the driving. There were fifteen of us crammed into one truck heading north, with our bedding and food, and extra gas.

When we arrived in North Battleford, it was dark—no streetlights, no pavement, and no road signs. The farmer was unable to find the road that would take us to Meadow Lake. The road that he thought was the right one almost landed us all in the Saskatchewan River. But the

Lord looks after babies and fools. I don't know which category we fell under, but young as I was, I can still remember the truck coming to a sudden stop and seeing the black water rushing by in front of us. We spent the night in a horse barn. The next day, we found the way to our destination safely. The experiences we had as new and ignorant settlers were many. For the next ten years, we lived and learned.

Our old homestead

In the beginning, it seemed like the settlers did not understand that feed for the stock had to be put up ahead of time, in preparation for the long, cold, hard winter months. Years later, when people got together to visit, one man laughingly joked, "I guess we thought our stock could be wintered on snow balls."

My father and his ox team

The same seemed to be true about ourselves. It was as if no one had given any thought to what would be needed to keep us alive. We had not been able to harvest a fall crop before we moved, so there were no potatoes or vegetables set aside. Because we came in August, there was no time to plant and harvest before winter. Luckily, there were neighbours who helped out and an abundance of small bush rabbits and prairie chickens. The nearby lakes also provided jackfish, pickerel, and perch. There were deer in our area but most settlers did not have a proper rifle, and if they did, the shells were too expensive. But, by the grace of God and a toothpick, we didn't hear of anyone starving.

Oxen Team

For the first eight years, we farmed with oxen. If you could not already swear in three languages, you could by the time you broke the stubborn oxen to harness. Oxen were our only alternative since all of our horses had died. This might have been because the horses ate the slough grass where mosquitoes and flies had bred, and their stomachs were not immune to the larvae growing in the slough. Or another possibility was that their stomachs were still half-full of sand from the Prairie sandstorms. Whatever the reason, it was a hardship to lose the horses.

There was no shortage of work that needed to be done on the farm. When we weren't picking rocks, we were piling brush. One of the natives living in the area claimed he was a pilot. When we doubted his claim and asked him to prove it, he explained, *"My brudder cuts the brush and I pile it."* The native Indians were part of our lives. We

I Am My Brother's Keeper

went to school with them, and they were our neighbours—honest and trustworthy.

There never seemed to be a scarcity of jobs or chores. We would carry a pail full of eggs, packed in oats so they wouldn't break, to the local store, which was located about six and a half miles away. The going rate was four cents a dozen, which we used to buy groceries. We picked blueberries by the hundreds of pounds. The early crop paid five cents a pound and the later crops paid three cents a pound. We usually were able to pay for our school supplies and some new clothes with the money we made picking blueberries.

In the early summer, we would dig Seneca root, which was used to make liniment. When they were in bloom, they were like a carrot. They had a bunch of stems about eight inches high and a small cone at the end. After breakfast, my cousin and I would head out with a gunny-sack over our shoulders, a small shovel, and a lunch. We would work at gathering the Seneca root until the middle of the afternoon. We would dig up the roots and tear off the tops, then throw the tops away. After washing them, we would carry them to the local store where we were paid ten cents a pound for them. On a good day, we could dig up three pounds, which equated to thirty cents; fifteen cents each. We returned home singing, "*When I was single my pockets would jingle.*" In those days, a man's wage for a ten-hour day was one dollar.

There was also work when there was a forest fire—these could be frequent in the summer and were ferocious. The Forest Ranger would conscript every able-bodied man. The wages were fifteen cents an hour, plus board. If you didn't like pork and beans when you signed on to fight the fires, you did by the time you came home. You had to wait until Christmas to get paid. The government was broke and so was everyone else.

I took my schooling from grades one to nine in a log schoolhouse with a ratio of fifty pupils to one teacher. We did all the things kids did at that time. We played ball, had our annual track meet with seven other school districts, and before summer holidays, we would have a picnic. At one particular picnic, one of the board members brought a large white rooster in a gunnysack. It was his intention to add some excitement at the end of the picnic, so when everyone (about a hundred people) was gathered around, he tossed the rooster into the air. The rooster hit the ground running, using his wings to propel him faster. After about one hundred meters, he was tiring and so was the mob chasing him. Now it was time for me to enter the chase. I caught the rooster and took him home. And, you guessed it, the next time we had noodle soup and fried chicken, there was no argument about who got the wishbone.

Senft's Way—this was our school bus transportation

Our first school, named Ferris, was a log structure built in 1933. Soon there were other schools built; Morin Creek, Deer School, Rapid View, Makawa, and others. After I graduated from grade nine, I quit school and took over the running of the farm, which was often a necessity for kids growing up during the depression.

Our life as a family was about to change, following a tragic event.

I Am My Brother's Keeper

CHAPTER 4

A NEW LIFE IN CHRIST

A young minister, Rev. Paul Gelette, his wife, and two children moved into our area; about fifteen miles north of where we lived. They came from Pennsylvania, in the United States with a plan to build a church and start a small Bible college. They had been sponsored by a large Baptist church.

A Christian brother donated a quarter section of land (160 acres) to the Bible school. It was good land with a natural hay meadow and lots of trees, which provided enough building material. The local sawmills cut the lumber on a share basis, so all they really needed to buy were the windows and doors. A lot of the doors were handmade.

The mission soon took the shape of a small settlement. Living quarters with a kitchen and bedrooms had to be built, and barns for the horses, cows, and chickens. An icehouse and a root cellar were also needed. The mission had to be self-supporting.

A common kitchen, dorms, chapel, and school were built for the attending Bible school students. They would be able to accommodate six to eight students at a time. Rev. Gelette taught a three-year Bible course, and many of his graduate students became dedicated ministers and missionaries to Africa and other countries.

On Sundays, the mission sent out male students to nearby schools, to hold church services as part of their training program. The mission also built up a local congregation of its own. People within the surrounding areas, who could travel by horse and wagon or sleigh would attend. People who attended some of these functions received some very nice clothes. Even second-hand clothes were very much appreciated. In the Depression days, beggars could not be choosers.

Graduations and every holiday; Labour Day, Thanksgiving, Christmas, and Easter were an excuse for a rally. The mission invited everyone to come celebrate and partake together. We lived too far away to travel to the mission and return home on the same day, so we (and a couple other families) were told to bring our bedding and some food to contribute to the pot, and we could stay for their rally. A rally usually lasted two to four days, with services morning, noon, and evening.

In February of 1938, tragedy struck our home. My older sister Irene, who was a year and four months older than me, died. She had been in the Loon Lake hospital, and the people from the mission had regularly visited her there. They told us she had accepted the Lord as her Saviour.

I am interjecting this because it was such a tragic event, which so devastated our family that we all started to think more seriously about Heavenly things. At the Easter rally on the last afternoon, when the altar call was given, my two-years-younger sister Violet and I went forward to the altar to surrender our lives to the Lord.

That was the happiest day of my life. On our trip home after the rally, the sky looked bluer, the grass looked greener, and every bump on the road seemed to give me another shot of glory. My father had his preacher. That was my first thought: *Now I am going to be a preacher.* My sister stayed a faithful Christian until she died at age seventy. My story wasn't quite the same.

After returning home, we got together with another Christian family and started a weekly prayer meeting. God really moved during these meetings. The very first night, my eldest sister got saved and filled with the Spirit. The children from the other family that attended all got saved. This must have been the greatest mini-revival in the north.

CHAPTER 5

ANOTHER MOVE

World War II was on. Things were changing; men were joining the military forces, and my mother and father thought it was time to seek greener pastures. I was now fifteen, and once you were fifteen or sixteen years old, you were considered to be a man.

So in 1941, after my father seeded the crop, he had an opportunity to ride to Calgary, Alberta in the back of a truck. There was room to go along for my sister Lenora, who was eighteen years old. I was left at home, in charge of the farm with my mother and two sisters. The summer passed like all of the previous summers. In June, I graduated from grade nine and quit school. In November, my father came home. He had a sister, Lydia Tate, living in Three Hills, Alberta and had spent time in that area, harvesting. He'd found four vacant lots at the edge of town, at a cost of seven dollars a lot. He hadn't bought them then, but announced that we would have an auction sale and move to Three Hills. There was also a coalmine there, where he would one day work, as a blacksmith.

We had our auction sale; selling four horses, seven cows, and all the farm machinery and household effects. Everything was sold. We packed our suitcases, and after paying off a few bills, we had $250 left over. We bought tickets on the Greyhound bus to Vegreville, Alberta. My mother's brother, John Flaig, lived there. My mother and two sisters stayed with the Flaigs, while my father and I left for Three Hills. We traveled by freight train; here, I experienced my first lesson on being a hobo. Two days later, we landed in Three Hills, where we stayed at my aunt's place for about two weeks. It took that long for my father to build a two-room tarpaper shack.

The first Sunday we went to church, we met some retired farmers who had moved into town. They were only too happy to help us build our shack. They also saw my father as another person that would join the church.

One funny incident that happened while building our shack involved me and a box of mortar. One of the men was a bricklayer by trade, and he volunteered to build the chimney. He had a wooden box on the floor, about two and a half feet wide and four feet long, and had just mixed a batch of mortar. Leaning against the wall, were the four-by-eight gyproc sheets to be used to line the inside of the shack. They were stacked on edge and having nothing better to do, I started to count them, pulling them back one by one. Unfortunately, I pulled one too many. Gravity shifted and they started pushing me. To keep them from falling to the floor, I tried to push them back but the more I pushed, the more they pushed. Finally, I had to let go. I made a half somersault and landed with my back in the box of mortar, about six inches deep. There were five men working. All the sawing and hammering stopped. My father thought that all the sheets would be broken, but luckily none were. When they saw that I was not hurt, everyone had a good laugh.

Our house in Three Hills, Alberta

Now that the little house was built, we needed the basic furniture; a wood-burning cook stove, a table, chairs, and a couple of iron bed stands. The mattress problem was soon taken care of. We had a bag, like an oversized pillow, the size of a double bed. It was slit open on the underside with a flap to cover the slit. Now all we needed was some straw to fill it up. Across the road was a field with a fresh straw stack. Under the cover of darkness, we walked over the road and crawled under the wire fence to the straw stack. We filled our mattress pillow, hoping no car would come along, exposing our theft and embarrassing us.

Now that the furnishings were complete, my mother and two sisters arrived. We lived in complete poverty. A Christian man nearby had an egg-grading station. There were always cracked eggs and he would give them to us for free. There were several draymen with teams of horses and wagons, which they used to haul loads of coal from a mine a mile from town.

I had nothing to do, so one day I attached myself to a shovel. There was a drayman who was up in years, and after I helped him unload his coal, he gave me a quarter and asked me if I would like to have dinner with him at his house. He took a liking to me, or maybe it was his wife who felt sorry for me; she told her husband, Oscar, to bring me home every day. They had three boys who were in the military—two were overseas. So I had a good dinner every day and earned twenty-five cents.

After a while it added up, and I had a few dollars. One of our neighbours asked me to keep him company on a drive to Calgary. We were to drive down in his truck and bring back a car for one of our local garages. So I went with him, seeing Calgary for the first time. (The population at that time was sixty-five thousand.)

We had to have supper in Calgary and I had to pay for my own. The price of a meal was twenty-five cents. I had always heard that Boston Cream Pie was great so I had to order it for dessert. When we went to pay our bill, the Boston Cream Pie was ten cents extra. I cried all the way home over the extra ten cents that I had to pay for that pie.

One day, my unemployed uncle wanted to visit Calgary. The weather was fairly mild with no snow that winter. He asked me if I'd like to go with him. I agreed and we got on the freight train to Calgary, where we spent a couple of days. Soon after we returned, my father invited me to go to Calgary for a couple of days to visit my mother's sister and brother-in-law. My dad had met them that spring when he had gone there with the truck. My sister, Lenora, was also living and working in Calgary now. The freight train stopped every day at the coalmine, so back on the freight train we got and rode to Calgary. I was starting to feel like a professional hobo. Little did I know, this would be an important turning point in my life.

CHAPTER 6

STARTING A LIFE OF MY OWN

My Uncle Frank and Aunt Lily lived a short distance south of the stockyards. The freight train always slowed up there, so it was easy to jump off and walk to their house. The next day, my father showed me the city. The center of the city was about a three-mile walk from my aunt and uncle's home; walking was a great part of our lives. The city streetcar passed by about one hundred meters from my uncle's house. There were no city buses yet, only streetcars running on iron tracks. The fare was seven cents a ride or four tickets for a quarter.

Eighth Avenue was the main street of the city, so we walked down Eighth Avenue then turned left, walking down Seventh Avenue. On Second Street East, there was a tire shop, which will always remain in my mind. War was on and rubber was hard to get. Everything seemed to be for the war effort—no cars or trucks for civilian use were built. Only jeeps, trucks, and tanks were built from 1940 to 1946, so repairing tires was a good business to be into.

In the window of the shop was a help-wanted sign, advertising for a boy to work. We had just wandered into the shop, not looking for anything in particular, when the manager asked me if I wanted a job. The pay was $1.50 a day and I would have to pay my own board. They were managing a rooming house and would give me a room in the basement. I was hired. The room in the basement was raw cement on two sides, with a table, a chair, an iron cot to sleep on, a few nails in the wall to hang clothes, and a natural gas heater, (which almost gassed me one night, since I had never seen a natural gas heater before). Near the tire shop was the Canadian Café where I could get breakfast for fifteen cents, and for dinner you could get liver and onions for twenty cents.

My mother was not happy that my father came home alone. This was March 1941, and I was still only fifteen years old. She had married when she was sixteen and knew what life was like without a childhood, and she wasn't wrong. Although I would soon be sixteen, the loneliness of being so young and being away from home, a stranger in a large city, was something I'll never forget.

I never learned to play hockey, football, tennis, badminton, or any other game that teenagers would play. But I learned how to play cards (poker), how to dance, drink, smoke, and use the Lord's name in vain. How did this change happen? Well, the Bible says, in John 10:10, "The thief, which is the devil, comes for only one purpose; that is to steal, kill, and to destroy," and he works slowly, patiently, and methodically. I started going to church but the congregation was made up of mostly older people and they never asked me to come to their homes for dinner. I soon lost interest and quit going.

I quickly learned my way around the city. I started looking for another job and it wasn't long before I had experience in many jobs: the Alberta Box factory, the Palliser Hotel, the Banff Springs Hotel, and harvesting on the grain farms. The big money was made on the grain farms, but the work did not last too long.

One summer, I learned the masonry trade, where we built water cisterns and brick chimneys, and stuccoed and plastered houses. When I worked, I was never lazy; I always gave one hundred percent. When we finished that summer, Mr. Fred V. was sixty-five years old and said he would retire. He told me that in fifty years of experience in plastering, I was the best man that he'd had ever had work for him. There were also other jobs, the last being in the Turner Valley oil patch.

I was eighteen now and I joined the Army. I missed the overseas draft because I was about a month too young; they couldn't send you overseas until you were nineteen. I was sent to Kingston, Ontario to learn to be a radio operator. This trade paid twenty-five cents a day, plus $1.50 a day for military pay, adding up to $1.75 a day; the same pay the corporals made. All this money was basically spending money, since all my basic needs were taken care of by the military. You could take a girlfriend out on a date, go to a movie, buy lunch, then buy a streetcar ticket back to camp—all with a five-dollar bill. By the time I finished my military radio operator's course, the war had ended. I served in the Army a year and a half and was discharged in May 1946.

Army life 1944

Leonard Senft

Back in civilian life, we had to get jobs. No more free board and lodging in the Army camps. My friend Howard and I decided we would go to Osoyoos, BC. We decided to allow the CPR to provide our transportation. We rode through the Fraser Canyon during the night, and I thought we would freeze to death. This ended my hobo career; after this, I would ride in style.

CHAPTER 7

LOGGING ENTERPRISE

Bill L. and Gordon R. were veterans that I knew. Bill was an Army sergeant. and a mechanic in the Osoyoos cannery. Gordon was also quite handy with machinery. At the time, I was mixing the syrup, but this was seasonal and we would again have to look for outside winter jobs. There is a cliché that goes, "You need a sharp pencil to enhance the profit margin," and Gordon had the sharp pencil. Chain saws for cutting trees were just coming on the market but none were available in Canada; at least, we didn't see any. But across the border, in Oroville, Washington, we were able to find a good quality, second-hand chainsaw with a four-foot long bar. The price was $600, which in 1947 was a lot of money.

Bill was married and had a five-year-old son, Gordon had only been married a short time and had no children, and I was single and had the most money. So Gordon, with his sharp pencil, figured out what it would cost for what we'd need. A chainsaw, an axe, a few files to sharpen the chain, a couple of steel wedges, and a small sledgehammer, and we would be in business. Bill and Gordon were in the process of forming a company but they didn't have enough capital. I had the money, so they talked me into joining their endeavour. We also had a promise from a small logging company that they would hire us as fallers. Now the sharp pencil again came into play; there would be so many winter months to work, we would get two dollars per one thousand feet for falling, and by spring, our wallets would be bulging with money.

Our logging experience

The first setback was when the small logging company said they didn't need us, so we got in touch with another outfit a few miles up the highway, up Nicholson Creek. We got into a packrat-infested cabin, where we had to do our own cooking. Of course, Bill and Gordon's wives had to stay home. The timber was scattered and small, and after the first month, we got a paycheque for only twenty-three dollars... to split three ways. About three miles up the road was a Russian Doukhobor Camp logging for the Boundary Sawmill, a fairly large mill. They were doing their falling with crosscut saws, so when Fred A. saw us using a power chainsaw, he talked us into coming and working for him. Here they had a cookhouse where we could eat and a proper bunkhouse to sleep in. There were also some nice stands of larch trees, so we accepted his offer and moved over to their camp.

Prior to this time, I had written the commercial radio operator's exam (as opposed to the military radio operator's course), an eleven-month certificate course paid for by the Department of Veterans Affairs (DVA). I didn't make it on the first try, having failed one subject.

At Christmas time, I took a few days off from logging, and went to Vancouver to re-write the test for that subject. This time I passed, and soon had my Commercial Radio Operator's License.

Gordon and Bill got busy and built two one-room cabins, then brought their families up to live with them. Soon after Christmas, we had a tragic accident. Mike M., who had a Diamond-T truck, was hauling logs to the mill. When loading the truck, he pushed a log on the load in front of him with a peevee, a logging tool with a long handle and a spike at the end, and the log he was standing on rolled back. He lost his balance and fell to the ground on his back. The log he had been standing on rolled off the truck and fell across his stomach. We got him to Grand Forks Hospital, but three days later he died.

The next thing we knew, Gordon was down in Penticton making a deal with Traders Finance for Mike's Diamond-T logging truck. He asked Bud L. (who had also worked at the cannery) to take Gordon's place in our big logging operation. Because Bud was single, like me, we chummed together. To have him join us would be great. Now why Fred (the boss of the logging company that we were working for) and I were there I don't remember, but we were in the Midway bar and had a couple of beers. Then we got into the Diamond-T logging truck that Gordon was going to drive home to the camp. The camp was eight miles west and then seven miles north up the mountain.

All went well until we came into the camp. Gordon parked the truck near his cabin. While his wife, Sophie, was watching out the window, Gordon got out of the truck and fell into the snow bank. I didn't see this because as Fred attempted to get out of the truck, he also fell into the snow bank. He reached out to me and said, "Boy, Len, I'm drunk. Help me." I was woozy and I said to myself, "Two beers can't make me this drunk." But I got up out of the truck and helped Fred to the cookhouse just a few feet away. After that, I went to the bunkhouse just behind the cookhouse. Since it was winter, the bunkhouse was cold, so I bent down to pick up the axe to chop some kindling to start a fire. My head seemed to explode. There was a sound as if a motor was running in my head. I lost my sight and staggered to my bunk and lay down. I thought I was dying. Soon Bill came to the bunkhouse to check up on me. He told me to come into the cookhouse, where Gordon and Fred were drinking strong black tea with a lot of sugar in it. He said that we had carbon monoxide poisoning. Having been in the Army, we'd been taught all about poison warfare. It was thought that, as a last-ditch effort, Hitler might resort to choking gas, and the remedy was to drink sweet black tea.

The next day, Bill helped Gordon to find the problem that had let the poisonous fumes into the cab. Just a few more miles and we could have gone over the bank or into the trees and been badly hurt or killed. This was my second poisoning, and I later experienced another.

I think it would be safe to say we learned logging the hard way. Because the saw was so heavy, we built a hand sled to pull it to the bush. Our four-foot bar and chain seemed too much for the power of the saw, but a rescue came in a strange way. We cut a tree that fell sideways over the end of the saw and broke a foot off the end of the bar. Bill was a pretty good mechanic. After we filed the rough edges off, shortened the chain, and moved the handle ahead, the motor of the saw seemed to handle it fairly well from then on.

We were constantly getting the chainsaw bar pinched in the cut, so to get it out we had two iron wedges about a foot long; two and a half inches thick at the thicker end; tapering down to half an inch at the other end, and a sledgehammer to drive them in. We were constantly losing the wedges. One day, we laid them on a tree stump facing each other, and cut a tree nearby. It didn't fall where we wanted it to—and this could never have happened again in one hundred years—the tree landed right on the stump. One wedge went right and the other one went left. The snow was two feet deep and we never saw the wedges again.

We were now getting regular paycheques, but the spring break-up came early, and the roads got too soft to haul the logs to the mill. We disbanded our logging operation. I got one hundred dollars for my share. What happened to the chainsaw, I don't know. Maybe it landed up in some museum. I can just imagine people looking at it thinking, "Who could have been silly enough to think that they could have gotten rich with such a monstrosity as this?" But all was not lost. We learned how to swear in Russian and how to eat borscht soup.

CHAPTER 8

MINING EXPERIENCE AND MORE

Pete was one of the Russian boys with us at the logging camp. He became very friendly with me, so when we had to start looking for another job, he wanted to go with me. I had a 1931 Buick car, so we went looking for a job. There was a hard rock mine eight miles west of Oliver, BC We drove up the mountain and when we got there and applied for a job, the boss said he could use only one man. As Pete was quite a bit bigger than me, he was hired. But Pete had no car. Because he had to find a place to board down below in Oliver and I had the car, we decided we would not split up. So, the boss hired both of us.

At the time, they didn't have any empty rooms in the bunkhouse, so we went back down to Oliver to find a place to stay. We had to drive up and down the mountain every day. One of the motels opened up a place to accommodate us but soon there was an empty room in the mine bunkhouse and we moved in. We weren't there very long, and were working on the night shift, when the driver of the little locomotive jumped it off the track, and after getting razzed back and forth, it just stopped. The mine entry, called the "portal," was horizontal, so it was just a matter of driving out and over the ore lines and dumping the mine cars. The boss was just coming in the mine to see if everything was all set up for the night shift when we had no locomotive, and the mechanic was off shift and at home in Oliver. The control panel was just ahead of the switchbox, which was electrical, and ran off a bank of batteries, which had to be charged every eight-hour shift.

Everybody was standing around, wondering what we were going to do and if we would have to go off shift. I had learned some basics in electricity while in the Army, so I said to take the cover off that box. It was only on with four screws, and inside were two fuses as big around as Ukrainian sausages and half as long. Now what did we do? I said to pull them out—the ends were only blades. Now that we had them out, what next? I said to screw the ends off. When we did, we found that one of the fuse elements, a strip of copper, was burned out. The shop was locked up because the mechanic had gone home, so I said to find a good size of copper wire and run it across the break. It would run for that night and tomorrow, the mechanic could put in a new fuse. So, we went into operation. The next night, as we were going on shift, the boss came up to me and told me to take over running the locomotive.

To get a job in the mine, it was a must to get a medical exam and have an x-ray of your lungs, then have an x-ray twice a year thereafter. Breathing in rock dust can result in silicosis, and once it's in your lungs, it is there to stay—the body cannot expel it. This is a concern for everyone who works in a hard rock mine. I heard a few years later that the mine shift boss died of silicosis.

The mine was fairly high up the mountain and it would get pretty cold at night, while inside the mine, it was quite warm. So, driving out of the mine into the cold air with about three cars loaded and then back into the warm mine (this was on the night shift), I soon developed a cold, then bronchitis, until I was coughing and spitting blood. I was sure that if I didn't have silicosis I soon would, so I quit and went to Vancouver. What ever happened to my friend, Pete, I don't know—I never saw him again.

In Vancouver, I went to work for Hume and Rumble electrical company; they strung power lines.

I had some experience in this area because after the war, a lot of small villages were getting hooked up to power. Chilliwack, BC was building a permanent army camp and while we were waiting our turn to be discharged, the Army taught the soldiers different trades; I chose the electrical trade.

After we wired the first houses, we had to run power to them, so we learned to climb the poles—over forty feet in height. It never bothered me, but it did some others. We were given a set of spurs to strap to our legs and started learning to climb up the poles. My friend got about ten feet off the ground, lost his nerve, and put more faith in wrapping his arms around the pole than in digging his spurs into the wood. He came sliding down faster than he went up, but he soon learned.

Because of my experience, when I saw a sign at the Hume and Rumble—Electricians Only Wanted—I went in. My qualifications weren't enough, but they said they would hire me if I agreed to dig the holes for the power poles for a few days. I could go as a ground man, and in six months I would be an electrician. So, I had a job but never passed the digging holes stage. Others ahead of me had been digging holes for six months, waiting their turns to become ground men.

Soon, it was time for the cannery in Osoyoos to start operating again and as I had my steam engineer certificate, I went back to Osoyoos. I also had my radio operator certificate and my great desire in life was to go to sea as a radio operator. At that time, Canada did not have many ships, so the place to go was Great Britain but that required money. Luck seemed to ride with me—the steam engineer job at the cannery did not require two men. I got paid for eight hours and four hours overtime—I made good money.

By October tenth, the cannery season was over and I was in Montreal with a trip to Liverpool, England booked, with the Canard and White Star shipping company. After the war ended, radio operators were in surplus, and they wouldn't even consider you unless you had six months' experience. So, I stayed in London a month and then came back to Halifax, low on money. But I was in luck again. New York longshoremen were on strike and the ships were diverted to Halifax. With our names on the spare board, we got to work twelve-hour shifts.

When the strike was settled, I was out of a job but with my pockets full of money I headed back west. In the spring, I got a job helping a farmer put in his crop. By then, it was time for the cannery to start operating again, so I put in my fourth year at the cannery.

Osoyoos was growing by leaps and bounds. A new school was built and they needed a heating engineer and a maintenance man, so I applied and got the job. The high school kids were all bussed to Oliver, but the grade school kids came to the new school in Osoyoos. Now, the school board wanted an extra bus driver. Harold C., who was a good friend of mine and had been a Greyhound bus driver, got the school board's permission to use the bus to train me. With Harold coaching me, I did the test and got my 'A' Chauffeur License. After only a year, there was a posting for a steam engineer in lower Summerland at the Cornwall Cannery. I got the job and married Rosie.

Our wedding in 1950

I Am My Brother's Keeper

We had met at a dance. I had never seen her before, or perhaps just never noticed her before. As we began the dance, she told me her name was Rosie and we seemed to hit it off pretty well, dancing together the rest of the evening. Over the course of the evening, we discovered that she too had been born in and spent her childhood in Saskatchewan, only sixteen miles from me. It is a small world.

In 2012, we celebrated sixty-two years of marriage. When we were first married, Rosie worked as an apple packer, but at the end of the season was laid off. The canning season was over soon after that, so I was laid off too.

Me, and my wife and partner Rosie

We decided to go north to Prince George. As I was getting off the bus (I had my A Chauffeur badge pinned on my cap), the manager from the Prince George, BC cabs approached me and asked if I wanted to drive a cab for them. BC cabs had a total of twelve cabs, and there were several other cab companies that had three to six cabs.

Rosie was young and lonesome as I drove cab twelve hours a day, seven days a week. Prince George was booming and accommodations were almost impossible to find. We finally rented a motel room. When spring came, we were given a week's notice to move out. They were going to their summer schedule and would now be renting by the day.

We couldn't find a place to rent, so we decided to go back to the Okanagan. Lady Luck was with us again. I got a call from the Oliver sawmill for a steam engineer's job. It was a big mill and employed six engineers. We stayed in Oliver for three and a half years.

While I was working as a steam engineer at the sawmill in Oliver, BC, I started chatting with the watchman, whenever he made his hourly check of the boiler room. We soon discovered that we both came from the same part of Saskatchewan. He was Chris D.; the man who had donated his land to Reverend Paul Gelette, to build the mission twenty years earlier. His son, whom I had gotten to know out at the mission, was now also working at the sawmill. As they say, it is truly a small world.

We had bought a lot and had just finished building a house. Bill, one of our logging partners, and his wife, Mary, were good friends of ours—a few months ago we celebrated his ninety-sixth birthday. Gordon, the other partner, also came to the party. He was quite an entrepreneur and was involved in several businesses, eventually retiring with a healthy bank account. Bill and Mary moved to Kettle Valley where they got a Veteran's Land Act farm and a small cattle ranch. On the same road, up the mountain a couple of miles, there was a ranch that came up for sale, which they persuaded us to buy.

CHAPTER 9

THE RANCH

Before we get to the ranch experience, I want to relate another poisoning experience I had that all but cost me my life because of my stubbornness.

It was the second year I was working in the Oliver sawmill, and I was on the graveyard shift. It was in the summertime and hot, hot, hot. At 2:00 a.m. it was time to eat our lunch. Rose was young and inexperienced and had made my lunch using some leftover canned salmon, as we did not have a fridge to store the leftovers. Canned salmon must all be eaten at once, and what is left over you throw out (at least that is what the doctor had told me). And worse yet, she mixed the salmon with a sandwich spread that had chopped-up dill pickle in it, which helped to mask the taste.

Now, the three boilers in the boiler room were fired with Dutch ovens. These ovens were under our feet, although there was a heavy layer of cement and also a steel plate over them, which we had to walk on. We always had to wear shoes with heavy soles. So, inside the boiler room, summer or winter, it was always very hot. That's all the salmon needed to start the bacteria working. I ate half a sandwich, but it tasted so sharp that I left the rest, and lucky I did. Before I went home from the shift, the pain and cramps were almost more than I could bear. My wife's first reaction was to want to phone the doctor. Why I didn't want her to, I don't know; our medical was covered by the mill. But because of my stubbornness, I said it would go away. When we grew up, no one went to the doctor, unless you were nearly dead, and to go to the hospital meant you usually died. This was my mindset.

As we were raised in the Depression years, and there was always a self-styled midwife who seemed to have homemade remedies, I suffered like never before. My stomach muscles cramped hard like a fist. It was 4:00 p.m. when my wife Rose finally phoned the doctor, just as he was about to close the office. Now I had to go. When I got there, the doctor got angry. He informed me that I should have come in the morning and we could've had my stomach pumped. Now, it had been more than fourteen hours and the poison had gone through my intestines and burnt the lining so bad it would take days to heal. So, I lived on soup and puddings for the next two weeks. This was my third poisoning experience.

Being a veteran, I got the ranch through the Veterans Land Act. The contract was the same for all veterans. You would get started with $6000; $1200 was a free gift called a gratuity and the balance of $4800 was a loan to be paid back in twenty years at three-percent interest, which really was a pretty good start.

This was 1954 and things were a lot cheaper. A new John Deere tractor was only $1200 and 500 acres of land was $4200. The logging companies were always out looking to buy private timber. Years earlier, the cream of the timber had been logged off; nevertheless, there was still quite a bit of timber on my land, and I was able to sell enough of it to more than pay off the place. The Veterans Land Act officer, who acted as an advisor and overseer, suggested I spend the money on a sprinkler irrigation system, as I had over twenty acres on the flat. With irrigation, we could get two cuttings of hay in one season. A creek ran by our house, which was fortunate because we had to go up the creek several hundred yards to get the forty-pound pressure needed to drive the sprinklers, and we also had running water for the house.

On July 9, 1954, we moved down to the ranch. My first job was to re-shingle the house with cedar shingles. It was a good house built of lumber (painted yellow) and all the barns were built of lumber, as well.

Years earlier, there had been a dairy farm operating there, with big hay barns built out of logs. The ranch was actually three ranches amalgamated, and across the creek was a fine log building, which to me, had the status of a mansion. This really was an asset and a few years later, when our house burnt down, we took up residence in it until I built a new house.

Life on the ranch

One of the real major jobs was building the fences. It was a never-ending job. As time passed, the ends of the posts had rotted off because they were planted two and a half feet into the ground. We cut dry larch trees into fence posts about seven feet long, and then we split them up into the diameter that we wanted. A couple of gas drums with one end cut out, and filled with creosote and used crankcase oil, was used to soak the ends of the posts for several days. There was never a time that the barrels were empty; we had miles of fences to keep up. Next, the crops had to be cultivated and seeded, mostly into alfalfa, which gave a pretty good yield of tons to the acre. I had money then to buy stock—the average price was about a hundred dollars a cow. We had some cash from the sale of our house in Oliver, and for every hundred dollars I could get together, I bought another cow. We had a range permit for forty-five cows, and at the time, the Cattlemen's Association required that we have a registered bull and that all cattle had to be branded. So, we bought a registered bull and branded our cattle with KV, on the left shoulder.

Rock Creek is thirty-one miles east of Osoyoos, and our ranch was another seven miles north and east. The first fall after our move to Rock Creek, men that I knew came into the area to buy Christmas trees; each one trying to outbid the other in price. The big Christmas tree companies were in Kamloops.

One big one was Kirk Christmas Tree Company, and they would ship the trees across the line to the U.S. by boxcar-loads. I soon figured out if competition to buy our trees was so interesting to these men and they were only buying for these big companies, there had to be some money in it. So, I went to Kamloops and contacted Kirk Christmas Tree Company. They were happy to strike up a deal with me to buy one carload of trees each fall. I would have to go to our local Forestry to get a little book teaching how to grade Christmas trees, write a test, and learn how to manifest the trees. (The government collects royalties on Christmas trees as well as timber, even on private land.) So, I wrote the test, and paid fourteen dollars for a scaling ruler. As long as Kirk Christmas Tree Company received no complaints from their U.S. company about our trees, they would give me an order each fall. So, for the next fifteen years, we shipped out a carload of trees each fall. Talk about a profit margin—in six weeks, we made as much money as someone working at the sawmill could earn in four months. This is what really built our ranch.

One day, while at an auction sale, I bought a registered sow with six little piglets. Soon after, I went to another auction sale. The sale was nearly finished when the auctioneer said that over in the bush was a building with grain about "so high," motioning with his hand. The friend who was with me was a prairie farmer. He was a bit of a comedian, and he said very loudly, "That's only about five or six bushels." This would be about three hundred pounds. No one was bidding, and I didn't want to check it out, so I bought it for thirteen dollars. When I hauled it home, there were about two and a half tons of oats. Soon, I had ten brood sows and a boar.

Being raised in northern Saskatchewan, we learned how to trap and skin animals and how to shoot. I started to collect old guns, and soon had a wall full. One day, a fellow I knew quite well came to our place (he was a gun collector), and when he saw all these guns, he just had to have them. He had no money but he had a flock of sheep. I soon figured out that sheep would make more money than guns hanging on the wall. So, we struck up a bargain—a gun for a sheep. He took the guns home, and I drove down with the truck and hauled my sheep home. Soon, I had built up a flock of about thirty-five ewes and a ram. I needed enough sheep to make up a load of lambs, as I had to drive them to Vancouver to Canada Packers.

I was involved with a few other ventures as well. Over time, I'd gathered up about thirty tons of scrap iron and copper radiators. I also did some custom butchering of pigs and a few cows. The cows were too heavy for one person to handle so I didn't do many but I did do a lot of pigs. There's a saying that it takes a good job to support a ranch but the truth is, it takes a big ranch to keep you in business.

CHAPTER 10

THE WIDOW MAKER

After we moved to the ranch, I always needed more money. As I had a nice pocket of very large pine trees, I could make a few extra dollars by cutting a few loads of logs. The small sawmills could not get government timber permits. So, you always had a sale for your timber. John 10:10 says that the thief, which is the devil, comes only to steal, to kill, and to destroy. I had cut down a large pine tree and had stepped back from the stump. I was holding my saw and had the blade turned sideways, when a limb broke off about ten or twelve feet long and about five inches thick. It fell in front of the saw and hit so hard that it bent the blade of the saw up about thirty degrees, and, of course, the saw blew out of my hands and hit the dirt. If I had not stepped back, that limb could've hit me on the head and killed me instantly. This is what they call a "widow maker." That bar was made of hard steel and no amount of hammering could straighten it out, so I had to buy a new blade. Chain saws were still so expensive; it cost two days' wages to buy a new blade.

Sometime later, I was working on one of these trees, carrying some choker's cables you fasten to the end of a log so the cat can hook onto them and yard the logs out to the deck. The cat skinner was trying to get through to the logs I was hooking up. All of a sudden, I felt a bang on my head, and I saw a cluster of multi-coloured stars. I was lying on my back when Jimmy got the cat in and I said that the tree had hit me on the head. It was what we called a dry snag. It was about twelve inches in diameter and quite high. Jimmy said that he had tried to miss it but that the cat had just kind of bounced over, caught it with the corner of its blade, and over it went. Well, my jaw was so sore, I could not eat properly for several days. Today, the x-rays show I have a badly kinked vertebra in my neck. I could write of many incidents where I escaped death by a hair's breadth, but I will tell of just one more.

We had had a house fire (I will elaborate later), and I was going to rebuild in a slightly different area. The twelve-foot by twelve-foot basement was in the wrong place and the cement was too thick to break up, so the easiest thing to do was to fill it up with dirt. I had a small scoop on the three-point hitch on the back of the tractor, which lowered and lifted with the hitch. So, I would back into a bank to load the dirt and then drive over to the hole. There I'd back up, and with the hydraulic, dump it into the hole. It got full at the front where I was dumping, and the dirt was sliding down to the far end. The dirt from the front of the bank was at quite an angle as well. This time, I didn't get stopped quickly enough and the back wheels of the tractor jumped over the four-inch wall left from the foundation.

I knew I was in real trouble and unsure as to how to get the tractor out. As soon as I backed over the wall, with the dirt still soft, the big tractor wheels sank down a few inches. Now I was sitting at a real angle; if the tractor continued to roll back, I'd be in the bottom with the tractor on top of me. The first thing I could think of to do was to dump the scoop. I set the brakes and tried to stay cool. Finally, I had to do something and I was afraid to try to climb out of the tractor. So, I put it in the lowest gear and opened the gas throttle as much as I dared, hoping the motor would not stall. As I slowly released the brake and let out the clutch, the big lugs on the tractor tires gripped the cement wall and the tractor pulled itself out, much to my relief.

CHAPTER 11

OUR HOUSE FIRE

While we lived in Oliver, the friendly stork delivered us two bundles of joy—Vern and Ken. So when we moved to the ranch, we had two boys; Vern was two and a half years old and Ken was nine months old. The stork soon found his way to our ranch and delivered two more babies, Sharon and Fred—four children in four years. We don't claim any record but this has to be a pretty good average. We discouraged the stork from coming again and this was our family until they grew up and started to leave home. We then took in two native babies and raised them; Florence and Shirley, who were sisters. My family now includes twelve grandchildren and five great-grandchildren.

From left to right: Foster-daughter Florence, daughter
Sharon, wife Rosie, me, sons Vern, Ken, and Fred

As the children grew up, they had to go to school and since we were beyond the three- mile limit, the school board paid us mileage to drive them to school and back home again. When the number of children in the area became eight or more, the school board had to provide a school bus. When two more families moved up the road above our place, we had our eight children. As I had a class 'A' chauffeur license, I was hired to drive the bus and drove for two years. Then, the two new families moved out. The neighbour had two children, so we drove them, as well as ours, and they gave us the mileage cheque. In the winter months, because the road above us was quite steep and our neighbour had a four-wheel-drive vehicle, he would drive and we would give him the mileage cheque.

Our children were our life; my wife's dream before we got married had been to work in an orphanage with children. We were always a tight-knit family and if we couldn't go somewhere with the children, then we just didn't go there. If you don't let your children down, they won't let you down. We had no problems—no police ever came to our door because of the children and even today, none of them smoke or drink or were ever on drugs. When they graduated from grade twelve, I bought each of them a car.

Old Jake, an old man who had lost his driver's license, would come down to our place, and I drove him around. He was well into his seventies and his last ambition was to see the Calgary Stampede. I told him that this summer, come July first, I would take him to the Calgary Stampede. My mother and father lived in Calgary so we would have a place to stay, and I would bring along the two boys; Vern, now seven, and Ken, five and a half. We would have a great visit with the grandparents. When we got back, I would send Rosie and the other two children, Sharon and Fred, to Calgary. So, everyone was looking forward to a holiday in July.

On Saturdays, we quit working in the early afternoon. As Osoyoos was only thirty-seven miles from the ranch, we took a gallon-cooler full of lemonade and in Osoyoos, bought some sliced bologna and a pan of iced buns. After we swam in the lake, we had a picnic lunch and then went to Uncle Leo's orchard—he was Rosie's uncle. We picked fruit for ourselves and also for Uncle Leo and Aunt Rose.

In the spring, Uncle Leo would come to our ranch and take home a load of cow manure for his ground crop of tomatoes and cucumbers. He grew the nicest big tomatoes, and one lady came regularly to buy some from him. One day, she asked him why his tomatoes were so nice. He told her that he fertilized them with good old BS manure. She never came back again for tomatoes.

It was early July in 1961, on a Saturday afternoon, and we were going to go to Osoyoos, but I was wanted to finish baling some hay. I was at the far end of the field, when for some reason, I felt I should walk to the house. I just got through the gate of the yard when I saw flames coming out of the garage door. The car was parked outside. I ran into the house where Rosie and the three kids were having a nap. I woke her up and got the three kids outside and into the car, then drove down the road a little way and told them to stay there.

The garage was very close to the house. I had a barrel of gas in the corner with a loose pump in the top of it. The heat just forced the gas

I Am My Brother's Keeper

out. By then, the garage, which was only a shell, had burned through and an arc of burning gas went right over, landed on the roof of the house, and started to burn. We started carrying stuff out of the house— Rosie was really good when working under pressure. She grabbed clothes and bedding and dumped it onto the bed, then picked up the four corners of the bedspread and carried it out. I don't know how many trips she made but she saved a lot. I was in the kitchen, trying as quickly as I could to assess what would be of the greatest value to try to save. We had a kerosene fridge we had bought for $600, so that was to be saved first, and then the white-enamel wood cook stove.

Old Jake had just driven into the yard. He had been planning to go with us into Osoyoos. Well, he was a great help. Although he was a small man in his seventies, we got the fridge outside. We then got the stove, a washtub filled with dishes, and whatever else was handy. The fire was crackling and burning on the roof and I said to Rosie that that was enough—no more running into the house. Because we had planned to go to the Calgary Stampede and I was going to take the two boys, Rosie had bought them each a cowboy hat. She said that she was making one more trip to get their cowboy hats. She ran into the house and came out hardly a dozen steps before the ceiling came down behind her. There was a poof, a cloud of smoke, and a blast of heat… and her hair was on fire. She ran both hands over her head from front to back, and the fire was out. As we had been planning to go out, she had put her hair in pin curls. I think only the loose ends of her hair were on fire and so she easily wiped the fire out. Had she had a full head of dry hair, the outcome could've been a lot worse. I had many nightmares over this.

The local Forestry, four miles down the bottom of the mountain, saw the smoke and came up with a pumper truck of water. When they arrived, the house was more than half burnt down, and the ranger's advice was, since we couldn't save anything, to let it burn to the ground. Then there would be less to clean up after it was over. The first thing old Jake said was, "I guess that takes care of our Calgary Stampede trip." But I said that since we'd lost this much, a little more or less would not make much difference. So we went for a week and it turned out to be the best therapy for me. I needed time out to sort things out and look at the situation from a different angle. When I came back, I was ready to go at it and start a new house. We moved over to our log house, which was about four hundred meters away on the other side of the creek, and as I said earlier, it was a grand log house. The first thing we did was to fix the broken windows and clean it up. As soon as a place was vacant, the pack rats would take over.

The neighbours were a great help. We soon had beds, a table and chairs, and the Ladies Circle had a shower for Rosie, where they presented her with pots and pans. We built the new house pretty well on the original site. Our front yard was level, and then there was a four-foot drop to a big flat garden space below. With my tractor and scoop on the three-point hitch, I soon had a basement dug—the basement would be three sides in the bank and the backside would be ground-level.

I had a four-ton truck, which I drove down the hill to the river and loaded up with enough sand and gravel for the footings of the basement. I then went to Penticton and ordered the cement blocks, which they delivered, and we soon had a basement. I joined the Canadian Legion in Greenwood, and they talked the local mill in Greenwood out of a load of lumber, most of which was rejects, but I utilized a lot of it. We had $1000 worth of fire insurance, which the Veteran Land Act collected and allowed the money toward some bills. The fact that we had no electricity and therefore could not use a skill saw, meant that I had to do all the cutting of the boards by hand. But I did have a small, thirty-inch bow saw, which I used to cut Christmas trees—that was a great help. Since I built a ranch style house, there were so many more angles to cut.

The house I built to replace the one that burned down

At the end of October, I had to start cutting Christmas trees for six weeks, as I had a car- load to cut each year. Towards spring, we had the outside of the house built and fixed up the basement so we could move over. We lived there for a couple of years. The log house walls were all lined inside with V-joined lumber, and the floors with tongue and groove, so I stripped all of the lumber and lined the new house with it. It was a lot of extra work but it was cheap.

This was the fateful day I told you about. One night, I woke up in the middle of the night with the feeling that someone was hitting me in the chest with a sledgehammer. It was like I was breathing liquid fire. This was my first heart attack.

This first heart attack was followed by two more, several years later, resulting in having triple bypass surgery. But that night, I didn't know I was having a heart attack. I didn't even go to the doctor and for the next three days, I could hardly even get off the chair. Every time I so much as moved, my heart raced until I couldn't breathe. My breathing got a little better, and after a few days, I started to do a little work. Slowly I got back to more and more work, but I started rasping in my chest if I worked too fast, and it took about two years before I could breathe halfway decently.

This was my turning point: I was thirty-five years old, had no medication, and no doctor. It was only by the grace of God I didn't die. When I had the second heart attack, I had sense enough to go to the doctor. He immediately sent me to Kelowna for an angiogram, where they discovered I had had an earlier heart attack and had a dead spot on my heart that would never heal, though it wouldn't get any worse.

They would've sent me into Vancouver for a bypass operation but I would not go. The last heart attack was in 2005, when they said I was out of chances and that if I wanted to live, I'd have to go to Vancouver for surgery. I did, and they gave me a triple bypass, which was 100% successful. One year ago, I had a knee replacement, and it has been a complete success. The doctors were amazed that it healed up so quickly.

CHAPTER 12

SALVATION

Ten years have passed—time has gone by so quickly. I am driving the school bus. My run is eleven miles; one mile on the flat and ten miles up the mountain. I turn around in old Jake's yard, and three days out of five, he's out there waiting for me. He has a little job for me to do or wants me to bring him a loaf of bread—just some excuse for me to come into the house for a few drinks, and sometimes a few too many. Up until now, I have not said anything about my health and my drinking problem. My blood pressure was high when we came to the ranch because of my lifestyle, drinking, and working. I was dead serious when I said I was burning the candle at both ends, and I knew it would soon burn out. The doctor said that if we didn't get my blood pressure down soon, I would one day die from a stroke. I was on tranquilizers for two years and I did have my first heart attack.

It is 1964, and I am no longer driving the school bus. Things on the ranch are just kind of coasting along; my health is failing, my drinking only getting worse, my tobacco habit just increasing, and my swearing and cursing is something else. I am angry all the time. In the Bible, John 10:10 says that the thief comes but for one reason, to steal, to kill, and to destroy but Jesus says that He has come that you might have life and have it more abundantly.

Now I'm thirty-seven years old. We have been on the ranch for ten years and I take stock of my accomplishments: a five-hundred acre ranch, an irrigation system valued at $3000; a full-line of machinery— a John Deere cat; a John Deere tractor that has a blade, a winch, and a canopy; livestock—forty-plus cows with calves and replacement heifers and a bull; thirty-five ewes and a ram; ten brood sows and a boar; two or three horses; and a contract for a carload of Christmas trees each year.

We were not long in the country when one of the old-time ranchers told me that I had sure built up a ranch in a hurry. Matthew 16:26 asks, "What profit is it to the man if he gains the whole world and loses his own soul, or what will a man give in exchange for his soul?"

And here I am in the prime of life. Here I am sick, with high blood pressure, a drinking problem, can't get rid of my tobacco addiction, my language is just filthy—and I'm the young boy with a father who had faith in God for me to be a preacher, who had at an early age accepted Jesus Christ as my Saviour, and who had wanted to be a preacher.

As I said, I was always a wheeler-dealer. The Veterans Land Act officer was out one day to see if I was all right, and in conversation, I was telling him about some of the trades I had done. He said I was the darndest guy he had ever met for trading. One day later, he came out to our place and brought along his senior Veterans Land Affairs man. He wanted to show this man a good ranch; they liked to check up to see how these people were doing and if they were hopefully making a go of it. A navy fellow had the ranch before us and had let it run down. Then he just moved off and went back into the navy.

Using a scoop shovel to clean out the rooms, I cleaned up the house. I hauled two big pickup loads to the dump after I cleaned up the house and the garbage around the yard. My mother and father had moved out to Kelowna to retire. It was a bit of a drive out to Rock Creek and then to the ranch but they would come to see and watch my lifestyle. One day, my father said to me, "Leonard, if you want to go to hell that is your choice but don't forget you have four children and you will take them with you."

My children were my whole life, and from that day until I came back to the Lord, I never had a day's peace. I was sick with high blood pressure, and when I got angry, which was mostly all day, it would feel like I had worms crawling in the back of my head. The Holy Spirit started to deal with me as I assessed everything. (What profit a man if he gains the whole world and loses his soul?) What was I gaining in accumulating all this worldly wealth and being too sick to enjoy it? Matthew 6:33 says, "Seek ye first the kingdom of God and His righteousness and all these things will be added unto thee."

I soon saw that I had my priorities mixed up and was working backwards. The Lord allowed me to go down to the bottom in every area of my life, gave me wealth, and took my health. When I studied the life of the great apostle Paul, I saw how God had to have Paul completely broken so that he could be rebuilt. It says in Acts 9:15, "But the Lord said unto him, 'Ananias, go thy way for he (Paul) is a chosen vessel unto Me to bear My name before the Gentiles, and kings, and the children of Israel."

So the Holy Spirit started to convict me in every area of my life and each time I looked at my children, I couldn't help but feel guilty that it would be my fault to see my family in hell. When the Lord starts working, it often seems to us in mysterious ways, but not to Him; He has His plan and purpose.

In Rock Creek, there was an empty building that was at one time, a schoolhouse. Mr. George S., (we will call him Brother Siemens from now on), had a general store in Bridesville; twelve miles west of Rock Creek. Every Sunday morning, his wife and two daughters and he would go to the empty building, gather up the children, and have Sunday school.

There was a small Pentecostal church in Bridesville where there were regular church services. Traveling evangelists and special speakers would stop for a few days and have services. Brother Siemens lived in Bridesville, right across the road from his store, where he also had a gas pump. So, any special speaker would be put up for the few days he stayed, get his meals and his own bedroom, and when he left, he was given a full tank of gas.

The Marriott family lived next to the church; they were very dedicated people. Viola, the mother, had graduated as valedictorian from the Bible school. We were good friends. Their oldest son, Ron, was twelve years old, as was our oldest son, Vern; they were friends in the same grade, going to the same school.

Rev. Sam Jenkins came to Bridesville for a few days of meetings. Ron invited our son Vern to come home with him to stay the night and go to the meeting that evening. When Vern came home, he said, "Dad, you just have to go to that meeting and hear that preacher preach." It was Rev. Jenkins' last night and since we had very little entertainment on the ranch, we went to the service.

When Brother Siemens asked Rev. Jenkins to stay over and have two meetings in his Sunday school in Rock Creek, he could hardly refuse. So, posters went up—two nights evangelistic services in Rock Creek. Later, when Brother Jenkins and I became good friends, he told me that when I came through the door of the Bridesville church that first night, I was the hardest man he had ever seen. That was saying something. Before his conversion, Brother Jenkins had been a well-known figure on the BC coast—he was president of the Boilermakers Union and helped unionize many other companies. He was also a boxer and a communist. In other words, he was a tough customer. But God got a hold of him and made him a new creature in Christ. 2 Corinthians 5:17 says, "Therefore, if any man is in Christ he is a new creation; old things have passed away; behold all things have become new." Rev. Jenkins became a national evangelist.

His heart went out to me and from then on, he prayed for my salvation. He came to Rock Creek and we went to the service. God started to convict me, but we didn't go to the altar.

The next day, I was in my pig barn, shovelling manure into the wheelbarrow. I was so under conviction; I wanted things to turn around in my life. Every time I wheeled a load of manure out of the barn I looked up the driveway, thinking Brother Jenkins would come to see me. Brother Jenkins later told me that he wanted to come out to our ranch to visit but it was early in March with snow on the ground and two miles up the mountain, so he was afraid he wouldn't find our place and he might get stuck in the snow. He decided instead to pray; he fasted all day and prayed for my salvation.

Now, it was time to go to church. It would be his last night there, and for me it was now or never. The church building was full, with standing room only. Never, ever was the building that full of people again. God had His reason for everyone in Rock Creek to witness the conversion of Leonard Senft.

The church service was over. Brother Jenkins gave an altar call, saying that if anyone wanted to accept the Lord as his Saviour, to raise his hand. Rosie and I were sitting on the last bench by the far wall. Rosie gave me a poke and raised her hand, and up went my hand before I had a chance to think or change my mind. Now we had the invitation to come to the altar and because we were in the back, we had to go past all the people. When I raised my hand, I started to cry. I had not cried in years, and it was like a floodgate burst. Rosie was embarrassed and poked me, telling me to save my crying until we got home. But I was not conscious of anyone around me; I was going to get salvation. At this point, nothing in the world was going to change my mind. As we walked up the aisle to the front, our four children joined the parade, and we got saved as a family unit.

Rock Creek had something to talk about for the next few days— Len Senft got religion; the man who could out-swear a muleskinner and could drink most people under the table. People soon saw that it was not just a flash in the pan; it was genuine. A friend of mine stopped me on the street and said, "Leonard, you are the last person in the world I thought would get religion."

Well, that night, the joy of the Lord came back into my life. 2 Corinthians 5:17 says, "Therefore, if any man is in Christ, he is a new creature, old things are passed away and behold, all things are new." I felt like a bird let out of a cage. My drinking and tobacco habit were gone as if I had never had them—there were no withdrawal symptoms. But I had to learn a new language, for I could not converse without using swear words to express whatever I was talking about.

The service was over and we went home. I lit the gas lamp. As I stood on one side of the cold cook stove and Rosie stood on the other side (there is not much heat from a cold stove), there seemed to be a sense of comfort. I looked across at Rosie and said, "Rosie, I'm going to be a preacher." We went to bed but there was no sleep for me; I had company. "For we wrestle not against flesh and blood but against principalities, against powers, against the rulers of darkness of this world, against spiritual wickedness in high places." - Ephesians 6:12.

I was just glorying in my new experience and falling asleep when the battle began. The devil whispered in one ear, "You have made a fool of yourself—it will not last," and I believed him and started to cry.

Then God spoke into the other ear, "Yes, you are saved, you are now My child." The glory returned.

As soon as I started to fall asleep again, the devil was back, "It's not that easy—you're still a sinner, you'll see nothing has changed," and I started to cry again. Then, the Lord came back to assure me I was saved. This seesawed back and forth all night long; my pillow was wet with tears.

It was an hour earlier than when I usually got up; I had not gotten a wink of sleep, so I thought I may as well do my chores. I lit the gas lantern and went into the sheep pen where the ewes were having their lambs. We always had one or two lambs on the bottle—some ewes had triplets—or worse, sometimes one would die or simply reject the lamb. Once you bottle-feed a lamb, he will run between your feet, bleating, expecting to be fed. As soon as the lambs saw the light from the lantern, they came running and one ran in between my legs and tripped me. If it had been the day before, I would have kicked it out of my way but without thinking, I set my lantern down, picked up the lamb and cuddled it in my arms, actually kissing it. All of a sudden, I realized what I had done. Love had overcome my anger and I knew the battle with Satan was over, at least for now. But he came back again and again—he never gives up.

The next Sunday, I was back in the Sunday school, teaching a class of juniors. I started to work together with Brother Siemens. I drove out as far as seven miles, to bring in a load of kids for Sunday school, while Brother Siemens went the other way to pick up a whole load. Then, after Sunday school, we had to drive them back home again.

The night I got converted, I made a vow to God: I would dedicate my life to serve Him and I would do it for love; never asking or accepting payment for ministry. Today, forty-nine years have passed, and I have kept my vow. God is so gracious and we have never been in need. In the pages to follow, I will highlight my forty-plus years of ministry.

My parents had left Calgary, Alberta and came to Kelowna to retire. They were soon involved with other Christian people and had a weekly prayer meeting. One night, my father was praying under such a burden that one of the ladies asked him what his problem was so that they could pray for him. But he said that he didn't know. Several days later, he knew; I had sent him a letter telling him that I had accepted the Lord into my life. That was the same night he was praying under that heavy burden, March 10, 1964 between nine and ten p.m.

Kelowna was about a hundred miles from our ranch but distance is no problem to God. My father lived to hear me preach and I think I can say that his joy was full.

My greatest desire was to start learning to know the will of God and the leading of the Holy Spirit. The peace and joy I was experiencing was almost more than I could handle. Brother Jenkins' theme song was:

> It's a little bit like Heaven where I am,
> I am walking with my Savior hand-in-hand.
> He talks to me and I answer Him.
> It's a little bit like heaven where I am.

For days this song was ringing in my heart, from the time I awoke in the morning until I went to bed. I just couldn't get over the peace of mind I was learning to live with. My health came back so quickly that I was soon going in high gear again.

That spring during calving, I lost two cows and ten newborn calves. The devil was trying his best to discourage me and that kind of loss for a small ranch like ours was a major catastrophe. But every time I lost an animal, the words just came out of me, "Though they slay me I will not deny Him." These words are from Job, though at the time I didn't know where they came from. In the fall, we met all our bills and the losses didn't make a dent in our income.

As I started to give and give, my wife, Rosie, said that if I didn't stop giving all our money away, we wouldn't have any money left to buy groceries. But we gave and gave again. One year, Revenue Canada ran a check on all of our donations that we claimed and I was quite relieved when a big yellow envelope came in the mail from them, saying that all of our claims were justified. I let God keep books for me and we have never lacked or been in want.

In May, we had our district conference; it was held in Penticton and all the ministers in the province were to be there, including Brother Jenkins. He took me under his wing, introduced me to many of the pastors, and told them how my family and I were saved under his ministry. One of these pastors was John Nygard, a missionary to our northern natives. He was in his sixties and not a young man anymore, to carry the load he was under.

CHAPTER 13

PERILS AND BLESSINGS OF BEING A LANDLORD

The year following our conversion, we got quite a good return selling the carload of Christmas trees, which covered the two hundred dollars we were short to invest in some property. We had decided to buy five lots, which included a log house duplex, which was quite large and built in the 1860s. It was a historical building and had been the office of the Gold Commissioner and the Justice of the Peace in the BC Rock Creek gold rush days.

Historic log house

The historic log house was at the south end of a twenty-lot subdivision. At the north end, there were three lots with three small ramshackle cabins and a house. Originally, there had been five lots but two were taken out by a shortcut between Highway 3 and 33. A friend of mine owned the property and when the house burned down, he collected some insurance money. The three cabins were rented out for ten dollars a month each.

I Am My Brother's Keeper

Duplex House and Single Cabin that I bought in an Estate Sale

My friend was a millwright and he'd gotten a job outside of Rock Creek and wanted a quick sale for this property. But he owed three years back-taxes and it would go up for tax sale. So he came to me and said that if I would pay him the taxes that he owed, I could have the property. I quickly accepted. There were also ten lots in between the north and south parcels. Lots six to ten had a small cabin and a small duplex house owned by a man who had a drinking problem. One night, after having a few too many, he was killed when his car ran into the ditch while he was coming home in the dark.

The family wanted to sell the property, so I put a bid on it in the estate sale and got it. After that, lots eleven to fifteen were vacant, so I approached the owner, made a deal with him, and bought the lots where we built the two-storey home. As well, there were three empty lots I owned, next to the lots with the small duplex house, so I bought a mobile home, set it up on these lots, hooked up the utilities, and rented it out. I also built a small, one-room house with a utility room.

The log house was so long that I was able to divide it in half and make two small duplex units. With an addition that had been built on the north end, I had a triplex. There were now eight rental units besides the three cabins at the north end.

I will relate some of the perils. A man named Wally rented the centre unit of the triplex. He was a chain smoker and had to keep a window open so that he could breathe. All of the units were heated electrically and the renters were responsible for paying their own power bills. The power bills came in my name and I just gave them to the renters, which normally was no big deal—no one complained. Wally had been discharged from the air force and was "a brick short of a load." When I went to give him his bill, he wasn't in so I laid it on his table. This bill was quite large.

Later that day, I was going with my friend Bob to my shed full of stuff on the other side of the triplex. When we walked past the triplex, the centre door flew open and Wally, thinking that I had given him the largest power bill, came out screaming; calling me a so-and-so. He had a large axe raised above his head and he was going to cut me in half.

As he was about to bring the axe down upon me he stopped short. With a look of fear coming over his face he said, "Don't touch me. Don't hurt me." I was still half stunned. I told Wally to forget about paying me for the power bill and for any back rent but that I wanted him out in ten days. He went back into his unit.

Bob and I just stood there, looking at each other. Finally, Bob said that it was because I carried a different spirit than Wally did that Wally became so scared. But it still was not legal for Wally to threaten me with an axe. Bob suggested that I report the incident to the RCMP in Midway, about twelve miles down the road.

I knew the RCMP corporal personally, so when I went and talked to him, his advice was to put a notice about Wally's eviction on the bulletin board. If Wally left, I was to just forget about it but if he didn't, I was to come back and see the corporal. In ten days' time, Wally was gone.

Another problem that arose could have cost me my life but God looks after His own. I rented the small cabin next to our house to a fellow named Dave. Dave was a big man, getting close to middle age. His hippy friends referred to him as "Animal." But we got along fine. He even came to church with us and wanted to become a Christian but he could not conquer his drinking addiction. He would come to the house and show me Bible verses about Jesus drinking wine.

Dave was always trying to see how close he could go to the line before it became a sin. He asked me how I overcame my drinking problem. I told him that the night I turned my life over to the Lord, He took care of it. For a short while, Dave had a lady friend and her daughter move in with him. One afternoon, he and the lady-friend went shopping and asked Florence, our foster daughter, who was about twelve years old, to babysit the little girl. Dave and the lady were gone quite a while.

It was dark when they got home and they had been to the bar. When it came time for them to pay for the babysitting, they may not have had very much money left. Florence, having a mind of her own, wanted more money than they were willing to pay. In a fit of rage, Dave grabbed a package of frozen peas, threw it at Florence, and hit her in the face.

She came home, her cheek already swelling up. When we asked what had happened, she told us that Dave had thrown a package of frozen peas at her. So I marched over to the cabin. The door was open—I guess Dave knew there would be repercussions for his actions.

As I came in the front door, Dave came running out of the bedroom with a loaded rifle pointed at me. Then he stopped, put down the rifle, and made some apology about thinking that it was someone else that he had had an argument with earlier. Not too much longer after that, I gave him notice to leave.

Now we'll look at the blessings. After I'd collected many years of rent at thirty dollars a month for my broken-down cabins, one tenant died. Another man wanted to move into my mobile home, then the other tenant had an opportunity to move across the road to a larger cabin. So I tore down the vacated cabins, in order to build a decent home and have a well drilled. When the Rock Creek Clinic next to me built a new, larger clinic, they wanted my property for more parking spaces. They also needed my well for a water supply. So I sold the property for about eight times what I had paid for it.

The man who had moved into my mobile home died after having lived there for a few years. He left me his car, an older Toyota; his mechanics tools; and a microwave oven for my wife, Rosie. The man who moved across the road became my good friend and I looked after him for over twenty years. He was an Austrian and had no relatives in Canada. He always referred to me as his brother and when he died, he left me his bank account.

CHAPTER 14

MY INTRODUCTION TO NATIVE MINISTRY

Pastor Nygard had built four churches with his own money; fishing when the season was on and beachcombing to earn the money. He was always checking around for someone interested enough to come and help him. God graciously works through people to answer prayers and to put the right people across their paths. I got into Brother Nygard's life and we became the best of friends, working together on several jobs.

There was a general store in Rock Creek, owned by Owen Wheeler. It was a family operation with one son, Wes, in charge of the gas and bulk plant and Perry, the other son, operating the meat department. Owen's wife, Lucille, was the clerk, and Kathy, the daughter, ran the post office. They all had their own homes, and I was their handyman. I did any kind of carpenter work that they wanted done and at times, drove the gas truck. When they built a new store, I helped tear the old store down and also did a lot of work in the new one, building shelves and painting.

There was quite a large warehouse beside the new store, which they wanted torn down. They asked me to tear it down for wages, of course, and said that I could keep all of the lumber that I could salvage. I could always use lumber on the ranch. So there I was, up in the attic pulling nails out and pulling down the building, when I heard someone below me. "Hello, Brother Len!" I looked down to see a half-bald man looking up at me. It was none other than Brother Nygard. So, why was he coming to see me? All I knew of him I had learned when I had been introduced to him a few days earlier at the Penticton conference.

I came down to him and after shaking hands, he told me that the next week, he was going up to Alert Bay to overhaul a gospel boat being used for native evangelism. He asked me if I would like to come. This completely caught me off guard. I did not know what to say; in my heart I really wanted to go but I had a ranch to look after. I said I would have to ask Rosie, so he suggested we go talk to her. We lived seven miles from Rock Creek, so we got into my truck and drove home.

First, I introduced Rosie to Brother Nygard, then I started to explain that there was really nothing urgent to be done on the ranch and that it was too early to run out the sprinklers. I don't know what got into her that day but she said that I could go and that she could manage for a couple of weeks on her own. So we drove back to Rock Creek. Now there was the problem of how much it would cost. A return trip on the Greyhound to Vancouver, then a return trip to Port Hardy, on the far side of Vancouver Island, would cost about sixty dollars and I didn't have two nickels to rub together. I had to do some thinking. Brother Nygard gave me a date during the next week and the time the bus was to leave Penticton; if I decided to come, I was to meet him there. I went back to work.

I had a bunch of wiener pigs for sale, and I had a nice dapple-gray stud horse. People would bring mares up to have them bred and sometimes I would let them just pay me when they could. While I was working away, someone came and wanted to buy some little pigs. Soon, someone else stopped and wanted to pay his breeding bill. So as it was, when I went home, I had a promise of ninety dollars. I took it as God's will for me to go. After all, who had told Brother Nygard where I lived and where to find me in Rock Creek? So, I went to meet Brother Nygard at the appointed time, in Penticton, and spent the next two weeks with him. To spend two weeks with Brother Nygard was an experience in itself, and I got three years of Bible school training in those two weeks. I was so hungry to learn about the Bible and to get started into the ministry I had dedicated my life to. I kept asking him questions and he was willing to answer and explain.

His mission on this trip was to go to Port Hardy at the north end of Vancouver Island, pick up the gospel boat, and sail it to Alert Bay, to a small island where there was a shipyard equipped to refit the gospel boat. Also at Alert Bay, was one of the churches he had built and because of Brother Nygard's interest in working with natives, the shipyard gave him free access to use of the yard and its equipment.

We arrived at Port Hardy in the evening and stayed the night with the minister of the church, (which Brother Nygard had also built). It was evening when we arrived and while we were walking to the church, I heard a chorus of frogs—it was kind of a swampy area. I asked Brother Nygard how we were going to get any sleep that night. Brother Nygard, with quite a sense of humour, responded, "Don't worry, Brother Len. There will be no noise tomorrow." And I said, "Oh, why not?" Brother Nygard replied, "Can't you hear them? They are ALL croaking tonight!" I think that the frogs were all rejoicing because Brother Nygard had come.

The next morning, we picked up the gospel boat and started to sail to Alert Bay, which was about forty or fifty kilometers away. Once we got well out into the ocean, the motor quit and in no way could we get it started. All at once, I realized we did not have any drinking water with us and I developed a thirst. But before I became panicky, a boat saw us, came over, hooked onto our boat, and towed us to Port McNeill.

The tide was out and we had to anchor fifteen meters from the shore. The water was just shallow enough that one could wade through to the shore in rubber boots. A boat always carries one pair of rubber boots but there were two of us. The boots fit Brother Nygard so he put them on and told me to hop onto his back. Luckily, I wasn't as heavy as I am now and he piggybacked me to shore. There was a Christian native family there, friends of Brother Nygard, so we stayed the night with them, sharing together an evening of Bible study and prayer. Peter M. happened to be at Port McNeill and since he had a boat and was going over to Alert Bay the next day, he towed us over not many kilometers.

While in the shipyard, I got some marine teaching. First, we got the boat up high and dry and scraped all the barnacles off. I never knew there were worms and lice in the water, attacking the underside of the boat. Teredo worms, the size of a pencil, drill neat, round holes into the wood. To repair this, you have to buy round dowels and drive them into the holes, then cut them off. But the lice need a different treatment. They start like an anthill in one place and chew up the wood into slivers. There was a patch about eight inches by twelve inches to get rid of. We used a blowtorch on them and they were soon burnt to a crisp. Then we mixed a rich mixture of cement and soda, plastered the patch over, and gave it a good coat of marine paint.

We spent two weeks refitting the boat. It needed the main bearing for the propeller shaft and because of my experience working around machinery, I showed Brother Nygard how to pour a Babbitt bearing. This was only the day shift. There was also a night shift but it was only up at the church. This was also a church that Brother Nygard had built, which included living quarters. Any friend of Brother Nygard's was the community's friend, so I was well received and being raised in northern Saskatchewan among the natives, I was completely at home. There were two services on Sunday, then a couple of evening services during the week and boy, could they worship loudly and boisterously. It was almost to the point of a full-fledged powwow. One service, they asked me to speak. It was still early in my Christian walk but I told them a story, concluding that where I came from, there were no fish. I prayed that the Lord would lay it upon someone's heart to drop off a few fish at the parsonage. The next day, fish came. I was told that's exactly how to deal with the natives. If you ask them for anything, then it is their pleasure to give it, whether it is fish or anything else.

All too soon, it was time to go home. Some time later, I helped Brother Nygard build a parsonage onto the church at Port Clement, on the Queen Charlotte Islands. One spring, I took my wife for five days, along to Port Rupert on the north end of Vancouver Island, to the native's spring camp. This camp meeting was early in the spring, to start off the summer fishing season. Brother Nygard and I became the best of friends until he passed into Glory. He and his family lived in Summerland, which was very close to us.

CHAPTER 15

MY FIRST SERMON

Now, if I was going to be a preacher, I was going to need some Bible school training, and living on the ranch with a family of four children, I couldn't just drop everything and go to Bible school. So, the next best thing was to take a ministerial course by correspondence and I enlisted in the Peterborough Bible College, in Ontario. For the next two years, I read no books and no newspapers, only religious material and my course. When I graduated, the district credential committee gave me permission to preach, then a layman's permit, and finally, I was given a license certificate. This is as far as I've gone. The only restrictions I have of not being ordained are that I cannot use the title of Reverend and I cannot consecrate a marriage.

I have never accepted a salary for ministry and have, consequently, never paid into the pension plan. I have achieved my heart's desire to minister to as many people as possible and because of my adventurous spirit, to minister in as many different places and areas as possible. To say the least, God has granted me that wish.

Each summer, Brother Jenkins and his wife came to the Okanagan for a two-week holiday. They chose to come to Penticton, this particular year, because their oldest daughter, Gail, was married to George

Price, who lived in Penticton. This was July 1964, and we had been converted in March 1964. We were invited to come to Penticton to visit, as we had already met George and Gail. George had a sister, who was married to a fellow named Jim A., and they lived at the coast. They came to visit George and Gail, and we were introduced to them as Brother Jenkins' converts.

As I was sold out in my new conversion, telling anyone who would listen, I told Jim A. that I was planning to be a preacher. He asked me if I came to Vancouver often. I told him that I would be coming into Vancouver on the tenth of August, to deliver a load of lambs to Canada Packers. Jim informed me that he ran a little mission at the east end of Vancouver, usually referred to as "skid row"—all of the people who were down-and-out lived in that area. He said that when I got to Vancouver, to just plan on coming out to the mission to preach their evening sermon. So, I couldn't backpedal and refuse. I said to myself, "You blabbermouth. You should have been listening instead of talking."

Now I was committed; I could think of nothing else. What was I going to preach about, especially to this type of people? Then I argued again with myself—well, if I wanted to be a preacher, I may as well start at the bottom, and for the next few days, I could think of nothing else but what I was going to preach on. I had never preached a sermon before, although, I had been teaching Sunday school. And where was I when I got my sermon? You guessed it—in the pig barn shovelling manure. It seemed that every time God was dealing with me, I would be in my pig barn cleaning out the pens. This just seemed to become my prayer closet.

Man is made of three parts; body, soul, and spirit. When people say, "Well, the Lord told me..." they don't necessarily hear the audible voice of God but God puts words in their spirits, and these words can be as impressive as if it were audibly God talking. This is how God gave me my text to preach about: I was in my pigpen, shovelling manure into the wheelbarrow, to wheel it out of the barn. The manure was flying into the wheelbarrow and over the wheelbarrow; I was just churning inside. (When I get frustrated, I work it off physically—don't get in my way or you will get run over.)

All of a sudden, I got my topic. The Spirit spoke to me to preach about my own self; where once I was blind, now I see, and a calm feeling came over me. I said, "Thank you, Lord." In John, Chapter 9, we read the account of Jesus and His disciples meeting a man who is blind from birth. Jesus mixes up some clay, smears it into the eyes of the blind man, and tells him to go wash it out in the pool of Siloam. The man washes it out and is able to see. Everyone is happy for the blind man's fortune, except the Pharisees, who are the religious order of the day. When it's discovered that this action was done on the Sabbath day, their comment is, "This man is a sinner, he is working on the Sabbath," and the blind man's answer is, "Whether he is a sinner or not, I do not know. All I know is, I was blind but now I see." John 9:25.

I had my topic for the sermon. Now I needed to prepare the sermon. A sermon needs a theme, a body, and a conclusion. It must first glorify God, and must convict a sinner, then it must edify the one who preaches the sermon. So, I studied and prepared for my first sermon. I went over and over it, until I hoped I had it memorized, because I knew beforehand that I would be pretty nervous. The tenth of August finally came and it was time to load my sheep into the truck. Because it was August, it was too hot to load the sheep in the daytime, so I had to wait until evening, then drive all night—285 miles to Vancouver, to Canada Packers' meat plant.

My sister Lenora, her husband George, and their daughter Yvonne lived in Vancouver, so it was very convenient for me to go there and have a night's sleep before I went back home. Yvonne was a year older than our daughter Sharon, so I took Sharon along with me. We drove all night, finally getting to my sister's place. She was a true Christian, in every sense of the word, and when I told her I was going that night to a little skid row mission to preach, bless her heart, she was all for it. She said that when George, her husband, came home from work, they would all drive down to the mission. I was just overwhelmed with this extra support.

The mission was at the foot of Campbell Avenue in the East Hastings area, which was not far away from where my sister lived. When it was time to go, we all drove down to the mission, including the two girls—I would have the support of at least four people.

First Samuel 16:7 says that man looks at the outward appearance but God looks on the heart. Well, I hoped this was also true for small mission buildings—the outward appearance did not resemble a church at all and the inside looked like an empty shell with unpainted lumber. There was no belfry, no church spire, and no cross—just a small sign that read Immanuel Mission.

Inside, there were several rows of chairs, a stage about a foot and a half high, and a small pulpit, large enough to hold a Bible but not large enough to hold my notes. Behind the platform was a small kitchen to make sandwiches and a bowl of soup, and to brew coffee. The lunch served after the service was what drew these people to come, and once there, they had to listen to the sermon. When we walked in, the place was pretty well full, some fifty plus people, mostly elderly. One man had a white cane so I knew he was blind. This reinforced my sermon topic but I was a little unnerved—the man I'd met, Jim, was not there but his partner was. Finally, it was time to start. I was sitting on the platform, while one man was leading the song service. There were also some ladies there to make the sandwiches, so the song service didn't sound too bad.

"Now, our Brother Senft is going to bring the message," and Brother Senft was sitting on the chair, swallowing repeatedly to keep his heart down, and breathing in short, sharp gasps. So, I got up and walked to the pulpit, which was not large enough to hold my Bible and my notes, and started to read my text: John 9, verses one to twenty-five. When I started to preach, the first thing I noticed was that my notes seemed to be valueless and I lost my place. So, I just started out and a feeling came over me. I preached and preached. I quoted Scripture that I didn't know I'd learned and there was a warm feeling on the right side of my back, as if someone was behind me with his hand on my back.

I preached about how we were blind when we were sinners and how God opened our blind eyes; about the joy of getting saved and the new life we would have knowing Jesus. Finally, I was finished and experienced something new—I was so empty inside; I'd given everything. I didn't know what to do, so I walked off the platform, sat down on the edge, and put my elbows on my knees and my face in my hands. It felt as if I was going to burst out crying. I felt a hand on my shoulder. It was my sister and I'll never forget her words; "Dad got his preacher." The one he'd prayed for forty years ago while I was in my mother's womb and I'm glad he lived to hear me preach.

So, I preached my first sermon and went home a lot less nervous than when I came. If this was the anointing of the Holy Spirit, I didn't want to preach again without it. In Isaiah 55:11, we read, "So shall My word be that goes forth out of My mouth; it shall not return to Me void, but it shall accomplish that which I please, and shall prosper in the thing where unto I sent it." Nothing would please me more, when I get to Heaven, than to find someone who accepted the Lord through my preaching that night.

CHAPTER 16

CAMP FOR KIDS

We faithfully carried on with our Sunday school; we had a Sunday school picnic, a Sunday school Christmas concert, and the highlight was the Kootenay summer camp. There were children's camp, teen camp, and adult camp; each lasting from Monday morning until Saturday night. Brother Siemens and I tried to get two carloads of kids. We would leave on Sunday and usually have to feed them Sunday night because camp didn't start until Monday morning.

The following Saturday evening, we would pick the kids up and deposit some teenagers. But we couldn't get the same number of teens as children, with some working at jobs. So, when we picked up the teens, we would also bring some ladies to adult camp but our number dwindled here to maybe four or five women and never any men. The distance to camp was about one hundred and thirty miles one way, and the men could not afford to be away from home that long because it was haying season, and it was too far to go for a one-day meeting. The results were just great, though. For many kids, this was their first experience of accepting the Lord and over the next few years, we got letters telling us that they were still serving the Lord.

Now, I'd like to share my experience of my first adult camp. I was converted on March 10, 1964. We were on the ranch and it was haying time in July, when the camp was on. I was so hungry for more of God and I wanted badly to go to the adult camp but had to stay home and put up my hay crop. The last day of adult camp was a Saturday and I had to drive to camp after work to pick up the ladies. It was a two and a half hour drive, so I quit early enough to be able to clean up and get ready to drive to camp for the eight o'clock service—the wind-up to camp for the season.

After the sermon was preached, anyone who wanted to could go forward on the platform to pray. This was the only part of the tabernacle that had a concrete floor; the rest was covered with shavings. I was so hungry for more God. I stepped over to one side of the piano; I raised my hands to Heaven and called on God. I fell flat on my back on that cement. There was no injury or pain and the Shekinah glory enveloped me. For the next half hour, the glory rolled over me and over me, until I couldn't handle any more. I asked the Lord to turn it off.

Nearly everyone, by then, was out of the building. I got up to walk to my bench but my legs wouldn't hold me up, I was so drunk in the Spirit. I finally made it to my bench and sat down. I asked myself how I was going to drive home in this state. They had the canteen open longer than usual, since it was the last night. The ladies I was to take home and I went to the canteen and had a hamburger and a drink, then started home. One hundred and thirty-six miles, and it was eleven o'clock at night. I just floated home on angel wings—I had never had such a fast trip or one so pleasant.

As a young Christian, these experiences were so precious and really helped me to grow in the Lord and trust Him. After all, I was thirty-eight years old and I needed to grow up in a hurry; the Lord had a lot of work in store for me.

CHAPTER 17

BUILDING A PARSONAGE AT PORT CLEMENTS

Five years soon passed by. I had my Licensed Minister certificate and was pastor of the congregation in which I was converted. I will always be grateful for their patience in listening to me practicing my preaching skills. Rosie and I were starting to look into selling our ranch. Vern, the oldest child, was seventeen and going out in the summer months on jobs, and I wanted to get into more ministry. I want to give one more report on our ranching before I sign off.

The first fall after we were converted, as I earlier reported, I had lost two cows and ten calves. The devil was out to see me go broke. That fall, there was an auction sale at OK Falls. The rancher was selling a lot of his purebred cattle, so I went to the sale and bought one bull and two cows with small calves. I put the cows and their calves into the corral where I was weaning the spring calves of my own.

My feed racks were built so the animals had to stick their heads in while they were feeding but they were not built for animals with horns and all registered animals have horns. I came home in the evening the next day, to find one of my cows had gotten her horn stuck in the feed rack, fallen down, and broken her neck. I did not swear or curse but I was really upset. I said that the devil got the cow but that the Lord was going to get the calf. The next fall, I sold the calf with my other stock at the OK Falls auction sale. It went for eighty dollars, and I said, "Lord, here is your calf." We lived on the ranch for another four years and never lost another calf. God's faithfulness is just more than I can comprehend.

While living on the ranch, we met a man named Armen D. He was well off but had a mail contract and a small freight line, with an "H" plate (that is a freight line license). He would take about three or four holidays a year and taught me his business. He hired me to drive his truck and do his business for him while he was on holidays. He only kept the business for something to do, to keep him occupied. About the same time that we were contemplating moving off the ranch, he had a bad heart attack, so he had to quit and I bought the business. It really turned out well for me because most days it only required about four hours, which gave me the extra time I needed to go and do extra ministry.

For the next twenty-two years, I had this contract and when I wanted time off, my wife, Rosie, would drive the mail truck. We also had the Coca-Cola agency, and I would haul milk and ice cream, fresh vegetables, and any other freight. I had a contract with the Grand Forks CPR agent to haul their freight from Rock Creek to Beaverdale Mine.

The hours were short but the money was good, and there was always someone around to drive for me if the freight, some days, was too heavy for Rosie to handle. Later, when we got a full-time pastor, I could leave for a couple of weeks at a time and the pastor would drive for me. These were the times I would go up north to work with Brother Nygard and our native Indians. On one trip north, I went to Port Clements on the Queen Charlotte Islands, where we built a parsonage onto the back of the church. With Brother Nygard there were always prayer meetings during the week and church twice on Sunday.

Here is a little humour, again showing how God looks after his own, even in the small things. In order to get to Port Clements, you get off of the plane at Sandspit, then catch a boat, which crosses the inlet to the Highway, to travel up the coast to Port Clements; twenty-eight miles away. There was a lady sitting beside me, so we struck up a conversation. Now, I have no way to get to Port Clements and this lady, who spoke with quite a French accent and was up in years, said that there was someone coming to pick her up. (I think she was going farther than Port Clements.) Women's Lib was going quite strong at the time, and jokingly, I said, "You know, with all this women's lib, you're going to have to carry your own suitcase," and she replied, "By the size of your suitcase, I think you will be the one that needs help to carry yours."

Then, she said, "I'll ask my friend when he picks me up if he has room to take you as far as Port Clements." I had my ride. So, God again provided in the smallest detail.

One night at a prayer meeting, I met a young man who was a hunter. When we met, he started to tell me some of his hunting experiences and when I told him I was a hunter as well, he just had to take me hunting on the island. The deer were very small but so plentiful, there was no hunting season. You could shoot deer all year round. Jim, the young man was working for the local butcher there in town, so arrangements were made. On a certain day, he would pick me up, bring me a rifle, and borrow his boss's pickup so we could spend an evening hunting.

The evening came and we went hunting. There was a lot of logged-off area and a lot of roads. Because it rains so much, the second growth of trees and brush are higher than the stumps, making it difficult to drive off the road, so we just took the logging road. We didn't have to drive far and there, on the road, stood a two-point buck. Jim, who was the driver, stopped. I opened my door, poked the rifle out and bang, we had our first buck. The buck fell down but jerked and shook and as we drove up to him and got out of the truck, he made a few more shakes and slid over the bank. This was about eight feet straight down into a pile of wet brush. I was glad that the deer were small.

Finally, we got the buck back up onto the road, and I quickly field-dressed him. Then we loaded him up and looked for another buck. Not too far down, there was one standing near the side of the road. Jim took aim and bang, down went another buck. We fought our way through the brush, only we couldn't find him. We were hunting around and still no buck, when a little ways off to the left, stood another two-point buck. Jim shot again and bang, down went the buck. When we got to him and examined him, we found that this was the second buck that we had already shot, so we dressed him out and went home.

The people that Brother Nygard and I were boarding with were

Doukhobor and I knew from other Doukhobors, that they don't eat meat. So I told Jim to take both deer home to the butcher shop where he was working. I should not have been in such a hurry to give my buck away because it turned out that the lady did eat meat and was a little put out that I didn't bring the buck home to them. The lady was very blonde, her husband had very black hair, and they had two young daughters—one was blonde and the other one was dark-haired. The girls were in their early teens. I named one Black Beauty and the other Goldilocks and I had a lot of fun with them. To show them my magic powers, I placed a chalk mark on the table, placed my left hand flat under the table, then I hit the chalk mark with my right fist and drove it through to the palm of my left hand under the table. Other tricks I would show them but beg as they would, I would not reveal how I did them.

They also had an older son, who had a Volkswagen Bug and it kept stalling on him. I had a friend who had come from Germany after the war. He had worked in the factory where they built Volkswagens and was a good mechanic. He had bought the very first Volkswagen that came into our country and talked me into buying one too, so I knew a little about them. The father had a small logging company and a large shop, so we put the Volkswagen into the shop. Firstly, we pulled out the spark plugs and cleaned them up, then checked the ignition points and set the valves properly, then we adjusted the timing, and it ran just fine. Whenever we had to go someplace, the son wanted me to go along in case the little "Bug" would stall, but it ran just fine and I gained a real friend.

Reverend Dave L. was pastor of the church in Masset, twenty-eight miles up north at the end of the island. He lived there but came down to Port Clements for a Sunday morning service, then took me home to Masset for the evening service. They toured me around the island, kept me overnight, and took me home the next day. The congregation were all natives. After the service, I shook hands at the back and was introduced to people, including an older lady. All of a sudden, I felt such a love for her that I just folded my arms around her and gave her a gentle hug.

The next morning, when I was back in Port Clements and we were back to building the parsonage, I told Brother Nygard what had happened and asked if I had maybe broken some code of ethics of the natives. Brother Nygard said, "No, no. They would enjoy this affection you have shown her." Soon, it was time to leave. We went together as far as Penticton, where Rosie picked me up. Brother Nygard, living in Summerland, rode another twelve miles to get home.

CHAPTER 18

SUITS

Our Christmas tree operation began sometime in October, after a heavy frost set the needles for the winter so the trees would not shed. The weather turned nice and that meant Kirk Christmas Tree Company would buy more of our trees; as many as we could cut. This was the first Christmas tree season after my conversion and we had a carload ready to ship out. I felt the love of the Lord well up in my heart, and it occurred to me that if I cut down a few more trees, I could send the extra money to Brother Jenkins to buy a new suit.

That same day, I drove into the bush to cut the trees. The trip turned out to be an experience in itself. The day before, I had driven to the OK Falls cattle sale with a load of cattle. My truck had the cattle racks on. They were fairly heavy and the two sides had to be lifted separately and dropped into pockets. Next, the bull-board at the front was put in place and then the tailgate, which was separate. Because I had to haul more cattle later, I left the cattle racks on. This turned out to be a mistake. When I drove into the bush to cut the trees, I forgot the cattle racks were on. There was a large tree beside the road with a branch hanging over the road. As I drove under the tree, the branch caught the cattle racks and lifted them right off the truck. I had to stop and load the cattle racks back on. Before my conversion, I would have sworn a blue streak. But now I praised the Lord. From the beginning of this little operation of getting Brother Jenkins the money to buy a new suit, I felt an aura of glory of God around me and I cut a load of trees, singing in my heart.

The next day, I graded them, tagged them, and tied them up in bundles. When the trees were delivered and it was time for Kirk Christmas Tree Company to pay, I had $100 extra. I sent Brother Jenkins the extra money to buy a suit. Later when we met, he said that he didn't usually accept gifts like that but he knew that I had done it out of love. The witness to him was that his tailor, who normally sold him his suits for $150, would sell the suit to him for $100.

The Bible promises, "Give and it shall be given unto you: good measure, pressed down, and shaken together, and running over shall men give unto you. For with the same measure that you mete withal it shall be measured unto you." - Luke 6:38

I saw this promise fulfilled shortly after I gave Brother Jenkins the money for the suit. I had always fancied myself in a sky-blue suit. When I was young, before I went into the Army, there was a style of suit called the zoot suit—it was all the rage. I could see myself in a zoot suit with jet-black hair (mine was dark brown) and a hairline moustache that would make me look debonair. Well, I got my blue suit. One day, while I was visiting with my friend, Bob, he looked me up and down, commenting that I was taller than he was and that he was quite a bit heavier than me. He had a brand-new, blue suit with two pair of pants; the legs were too long for him and the waist too small. He told me if it fit, it was mine. When I tried it on, it could not have been a better fit than if a tailor had made it just for me.

The blessing did not stop there. When I was in Osoyoos, I went to the Modern Tailor store. The manager, whom I knew well, said, "We are changing our line of stock. I have a suit here that will fit you perfectly. I have to put it through the books as a sale, so if you are interested, give me five dollars for it." So, I did and went home with *another* new suit. It had patch pockets, sewn on the outside, and it could not have fit me better if it had been tailor-made. We had a church member, who was always well dressed and he knew clothes and how to wear them. The first time I wore this suit to the church, he came up to me and complimented me on my nice summer suit. God always give us the best!

God gave me another opportunity to bless someone with suits. My wife's aunt, Rose Wurm, gave me some of her late husband's clothes to give away—three very expensive suits, shirts, ties, and a hat. So I took them, not knowing exactly what I was going to do with them. There was an English couple, who came to our church. With typical English accent and humour, the husband loved to play tricks on people. We were good friends and one night, we invited them to our house. We had a two-storey house that I'd built in Rock Creek. The front was ground level with an entry door and two carport stalls, and around the corner was a staircase with another entry into the house

The house I built in Rock Creek

I asked Al to come down into the basement, where we had a bedroom, a bathroom, and a large family room, to see the suits from Aunt Rose. He said he could use one and picked one out. It was *another* perfect fit for him. He also tried on a shirt and tie, and even the hat, which surprisingly fit. Then he went out the basement door, all dressed up, took the steps to the side door entrance of the house, and rang the doorbell. My wife came and opened the door. With Al standing in the darkness, under the dim porch light, as stiff as a tin soldier, with a deadpan expression, my wife did not recognize him. By that time, his wife came to see who was at the door. For a moment, she didn't recognize him either. Well, we really had a hearty laugh over that—our little joke was a complete success. So, I ended up outfitting Al with two suits, shirts, and ties, and he took them as a blessing from the Lord. But I think mine was the greater blessing in giving—Acts 20:35; "It is more blessed to give than to receive."

CHAPTER 19

HAZELTON

My wife and I decided to go to Prince Rupert and by the time we were going through Hazelton, it was getting late in the evening, so we decided to stop at Rev. Jack and his wife, Erma's, place to say hello. Erma invited us to stay for supper and Rev. Jack insisted that we stay the night. We stayed the night and established a friendly relationship that lasted until Erma and Rev. Jack passed on to their Heavenly reward. They had ministered to the natives for over thirty years before we met them.

We left the next morning, with Rev. Jack giving me an invitation to come and work with him whenever I could find the time. I wasn't long in taking up his invitation. I loaded a few crates of cherries in a small trailer and spent the next two weeks in Hazelton. The natives accepted me, as I was Rev. Jack's friend, and they thought that Jack and I were brothers. Well, we were spiritual brothers but not in the flesh. We could have resembled each other but Rev. Jack was more than ten years older than me. I have never worked with a finer brother. I parked my trailer just outside the yard fence and went into the house for meals.

The last time I saw Rev. Jack was in Kelowna at our District Conference. I told him the thing that I remembered most vividly was breakfast at his place with raspberry jam and toast. They always had a large garden and the raspberry bush was the largest I had ever seen and the bread that they bought at the local bakery was just the best. They lived in an old house and Erma wished for better cupboards and more space, so I volunteered to build her some cupboards. We measured up what we needed, then drove to Smithers, to the Building Supply store, and picked up our plywood and arborite, hinges and latches, and soon Erma had some new cupboards and a new sink that we plumbed in.

Soon, I had to go back home but I did preach a few times and we had our midweek Bible study and prayer meeting. When I left, Rev. Jack gave me an open invitation to come back again anytime I was available or wanted to come. Our congregation was growing and we had built up a surplus of money, so we decided to have a full-time minister. The District had offered to pay "home missions," which paid a small amount towards a minister's salary. Most of the men of the congregation were employed at the Pope and Talbot Sawmill, an American-owned mill. They were making good money and tithed consistently. Our new minister was a young man named Rev. Richard F., who stayed for seven and a half years and did an excellent job. While he was with us, we built a new church in Rock Creek. This left me free, so I decided to go back to Hazelton.

Going on my second missionary journey, I was starting to feel like the apostle Paul. I loaded the small trailer with peaches, as heavy as I could and was well received in Hazelton. Once again, the Lord was on our side. The first morning after I got to Hazelton, while the women were dividing up the peaches, Rev. Jack started to tell me that one of the church members was able to buy mobile school trailers for one dollar each. There were several mobile school units available. A large central school had been built and all the trailers were to be sold and moved, selling each one for one dollar, just to make it legal. The people working for the school board as janitors had first choice, and Phil, a church member, bought one for the church.

The church wanted Sunday school rooms, and would move this trailer up against the church, over a basement the same size as the trailer. When the basement was dug, they found they had no one to lay the cement blocks. The one man in Hazelton who could lay blocks was working on another job and would not be free for some time. I told

Jack that I had experience laying blocks, having built several cement block foundations. Rev. Jack said that he knew that the Lord had sent me there for a purpose. The next day, we went to the church to measure out the trailer, because the size had to be exact. We laid a foundation sixteen feet wide and forty feet long. There were enough men with a couple of pickups to haul the gravel for the foundation, the sand to mix the cement to lay the blocks, and the cement mixer. A couple of days later, we were laying blocks. I just got finished laying the blocks when it was time to go home.

They sure treated me well while I was there. Phil took me moose hunting one day, and another day he took me fishing. I was also invited to an Indian powwow—that was an experience I'll never forget. There was dancing and every kind of wild meat and fish was available to eat. I tried a piece of smoked beaver meat—it tasted so bad I couldn't get it out of my mouth fast enough. Soon, I couldn't eat anymore but the salmon tasted so good that I took a large piece and put it in my pocket. The next morning at the breakfast table, I pulled out this piece of salmon and said to Rev. Jack, "Look what I salvaged," and he laughed and said, "You will be an Indian. Yes, you will be an Indian."

New Hazelton is made up of three different villages. Five miles north of the highway is Old Hazelton, which is the original town. Then, on the main highway is New Hazelton, and a little further down is South Hazelton. There are some other villages, as well. North twelve miles up the Kispiox River is the village of Kispiox, then up the highway, west of South Hazelton, is the village Kitwanga, which is a junction, and going north, twenty miles, is a village; Kitwancool. Rev. Jack ministered in all of these villages and was well known and loved by the natives.

When an Indian dies, the coffin and corpse are taken to the home of the relative who has the largest front room. The coffin is placed in the middle of the room and chairs are placed around it. The coffin cannot go in and out of the same opening of the house. If it is brought in through the front door, then it must be taken out a different way, perhaps through a window that has been removed. There is a vigil kept all night called a "wake." People come and go all night or sit all night on the chairs, while in the kitchen the women make coffee, sandwiches, and cakes to be served at intervals throughout the night. No liquor is allowed. The grave cannot be dug ahead of time and left open, because evil spirits might invade it. I was with Rev. Jack for two wakes.

An old native chief died—he had been a fine Christian man and the funeral was at Kitwancool, about fifty miles from where Rev. Jack and Erma lived. Because of the distance, we had to leave before the big celebration took place. We waited and waited at Kitwancool as the chief was buried there. Before the funeral service started, the grave had to be finished. The funeral was a new experience—every denomination from the different churches that are in ministry in the area was represented; the Salvation Army, the United church, the Anglican church, the Catholic church, and the Pentecostal church. I was also invited to sit on the platform and each of us was given a time to share. There were several hundred people in the hall. When we were finished speaking, all the people went to the graveside; each relative with his family walking up to the grave, and there saying last goodbyes. Their mourning was loud and vocal.

Now that the chief had died, someone had to take his place. Their protocol was that the eldest son of the wife was in line to be chosen. The last thing to be done at the graveside was for the new chief to put on the chieftain's robe. The funeral was over and everyone went to the big hall for the banquet, except our party. It was getting too late and we had fifty miles to drive home. This was one of the highlights of my ministry at Hazelton. The time had come for me to say goodbye. I had a business at home and two weeks was usually as long as I could stay away.

CHAPTER 20

FOSTER PARENTS

My wife Rosie is a real mother at heart, and as our four children started to leave home, in order to be happy, she needed children around her, to take care of. Our yard had always had children in it but the two oldest boys had left home to further their education and the other two would soon follow. Rosie's mother was working with the Social Services from Oliver, and she used to supply respite care for short periods of time. When two native sisters came into her care, the oldest girl, Shirley, being twenty-two months old, and the youngest, Florence, fourteen months old, my wife, the mother that she was, asked to take them home. Oliver is in another district than what we were in. Rosie got permission to take them home on a visiting basis and they landed up living with us until they grew up. Today, they are forty-three and forty-two years old.

The Foster Parents Association found out about us raising two foster girls, so a man and a woman came to our home from Vernon and Winfield, to explain to us the working operation and the benefits for the children, if we were to become members of the Foster Parents Association. They also wondered if we would form a local chapter. I was voted president and held that position for eleven years, until the girls grew up and were no longer supported by the Ministry. These were very interesting and informative years. The Federation of Foster Parents Association is national but we operate only in our own province. Our headquarters is in Vancouver and has a provincial executive, a president, a secretary, a vice president, and a treasurer.

The province of BC is divided into twenty-one districts or regions, and we were in region three. It takes in all the area from Vernon, south to the US border, then south and west to cover all the area, including Beaverdale, Midway, and Grand Forks. Then that area is divided into locals in the towns and cities. Each region has its own executive president, secretary, vice president, and treasurer. Then, the region tries to get as many locals as possible; one from each town or city. The local I put together was called the Boundary Local, which took in the area including Rock Creek, Midway, Greenwood, and Grand Forks. The chain of command now is: the provincial at Vancouver, the regional (they usually alternated one year in Kelowna and one year in Vernon), and the local (as many as possible). The meetings would be once a month at the regional level and once a month at the local level. The president of each local was to attend the regional meeting and there would be one regional representative to attend the provincial meetings, which were six times a year.

The purpose of the Federation of Foster Parents Association was to act as a watchdog over the children in "Care," which used to be called "Welfare," but changed to "Social Services." My wife and I had a good working relationship with the local Social Services in Grand Forks, and they would allow us to use their conference room in their building for our local meetings. We had an annual general business meeting once a year. The Minister or his deputy would attend, and we would put forth motions and discuss them, then vote on them. If they were passed, there was a lawyer present who would write them up in a legal manner. They were then presented to the government in Victoria—many of our motions were passed

We got vacations for the kids like summer camps and sports equipment, skates, bicycles, better orthodontic care, and more modern frames for eyeglasses. We were never out pocket money—our expenses and meals were always paid for and plane fare was paid for or mileage if you came by car. But our time was volunteered and not everyone was able to take time off from his or her job. We always had workshops at different points in the province and the mileage was always paid.

The AGM was held two years in Vancouver, then every third year it was in some smaller place like Kamloops, Vernon, or Prince George. It was always a two-day affair; the first day was workshops, several from which you could choose, and all foster parents were invited if they could come. All expenses were paid—travel as well as accommodation.

One of the highlights of my time with the Foster Parents was when they asked me to be Master of Ceremonies for the banquet in Prince George, because after the banquet they had some evening entertainment. I was the Regional Representative for two years. Twice I was sent to Victoria with a few others to learn how to put meetings together, to write up constitutions, and to register new companies. We were billeted at a hotel near to the parliament buildings, and each day, a parliamentarian taught us. We were all given the *Robert's Rules of Order* book.

One time, I had the privilege of being sent to Seattle, to the Child Welfare League of America, for a five-day conference and workshop, and I had to give a report to our provincial and regional people when I got back. Before our girls were old enough to go off foster care, we were invited to go to Trail, to a joint meeting with Social Services and the Foster Parents Association. We were presented with a written citation and a wall plaque for our contribution to children in need. Every opportunity I got, I presented the Lord.

In my years with the Federation of Foster Parents Association, I met many fine and caring people and always tried to give a Christian testimony. I discovered many other Christian parents. After all, it is these people who have the greatest love to minister and to give to the many children who need care and love. We don't see the many abused children, nor are we aware of the suicide rate among teenagers.

At the Child Welfare League of America conference I attended in Seattle, one doctor, who specialized with children's ministry, stood on the stage and cried as he told of the broken bodies that were brought into the hospital; broken bones and black and blue bruises. He said that one parent bitterly threw his young child down the staircase. One day, these people will pay for their atrocities. "For we must all appear before the judgement seat of Christ, that each one may receive the things done in his body, according to what he has done, whether good or bad." 2 Corinthians 5:10.

CHAPTER 21

HOSPICE SOCIETY

I saw an ad in the local Osoyoos paper, asking for hospice volunteers, and there was a contact phone number. My first reaction was to check it out—this might be another opportunity to meet people and minister to them. I contacted the co-ordinator and the lady was more than willing to have me join. They had twenty ladies and two men already, and wanted more male influence in the group.

First, I had to go through their training program, which consisted of ten, two-hour sessions once a week at the Penticton Hospital, in their conference room. We were still living in Rock Creek, so this would be a one hundred and fifty-mile return trip. I completed the ten-week course, which was very interesting, and I was taken on the team as a hospice volunteer; I got a red badge with my name on it. We had a meeting once every month, in the conference room at the Oliver hospital, and sometimes we would have special speakers, such as pharmacy people and doctors, who were always interesting.

We were assigned a patient who was terminal, and stayed with him until the end of his life. We were to build a buddy-buddy relationship with him and spend an hour or two together one day a week. If they were able, you could take them out for a coffee. If they had to go to the hospital, you would take them or bring them home from the hospital. But we were told that the patient was always in control—if he or she said it was over, you had to leave. We had two palliative wards in the hospital, and we were expected to sit with a patient once a week from two to four hours.

As I had been in Osoyoos since 1946, I sometimes would get a patient whom I had known for many years. As soon as they remembered me and that I could speak German, they really enjoyed our time together. I had been told I could not preach religion to them but this was an open door for me and as long as I didn't anger anyone, there was no problem. I would always ask them if I could pray for them, and the answer was, "Oh, please do." There was only one man, Walter, who didn't want any part of religion but he knew who to phone if he had to go to the hospital or needed to come home from the hospital. Dr. Cox would leave me some names of his patients to go visit if I had the time.

The first patient that I had was blind. He was sixty-four years old, and when it was discovered that he had lung cancer, he'd wanted to end his life. He used a small calibre gun and tried to shoot himself in the head but all he accomplished was to blind himself and he lived for the next two years totally blind. The co-ordinator made contact with him, and told him she would assign a buddy for him. She contacted me to come on a certain day. In between, he changed his mind and made it quite clear that he didn't want anyone to come. As we lived in Rock Creek, the co-ordinator was unable to contact me. I came and didn't know why I received such a cold reception. But I can be thick-skinned when I get to help someone and maybe get a chance to preach the Gospel to him. Two hours later, I left him. We parted friends and he looked forward to me coming back.

When I ministered to a Catholic, I would tell them that my wife was raised in the Catholic faith and it always opened the door to minister Christ to them. One of my patients' name was Ed S., and I soon led him to the Lord. Ed steadily got worse—his lungs were bleeding inside and he was sent to the Oliver hospital. I kept visiting him and the head nurse hinted that he was getting worse rapidly. One day in Rock Creek, I just couldn't get into my job. All I could get was, "Go and see Ed. Go and see Ed." So, I changed my clothes, got into my car, and drove to Oliver, to the hospital.

When I entered Ed's room, he was quite surprised; it was not my usual day to visit. So, I said, "Ed, I just wanted to make sure all was well between you and the Lord," and he said, "Don't worry, Len, all is well taken care of." I went home quite relieved. That night, the hospital had a fire in the electrical room. All of the patients had to be evacuated; some were sent to the Penticton hospital, others to the Summerland hospital. A few days later, they sent me word that Ed had passed away—the move had been too strenuous for him. I really felt good that I had that last visit with him and that I had been obedient to the leading of the Spirit of God.

There were many other patients that I was involved with. Jim M. was well off financially. His wife had died earlier, and he was in the Sagebrush Lodge in Osoyoos. When I came to see him, he had me drive him to Oliver to the café, where he treated me to a meal and was determined to pay me for my trip to Oliver. I led him to the Lord. At his funeral, the minister asked me to say a prayer over him.

One patient I was to meet died the night before our first visit. Bill R. was also in the Sagebrush Lodge. We had several visits, and one day when I came to visit him, they said they'd taken him to the Oliver hospital the night before, and he died before morning.

We moved to Kelowna and I left the Hospice Society but was soon involved in other ministries. It was 1999, and after settling into an apartment, I began looking around for some ministry, when I decided to check out the Gospel Mission on Leon Avenue. They were glad to accept me. Arrangements were made that once a week at noon on Tuesday, it would be my turn to minister for about fifteen minutes before the mission's clients could start eating their dinner. The midday meal was free. They also had sleeping quarters for about forty-five people. You needed to apply to Social Services to get this accommodation and if you qualified, you got meal tickets for breakfast and supper. They also had a store where people could buy inexpensive clothing.

I stayed with the Mission for one year and then I got involved in the Sutherland Hills Nursing Home, where I was a fill-in for Sunday afternoons and Wednesday morning Bible study. I was also involved in the church that we were attending (Rutland Gospel Tabernacle), where I taught the adult Sunday school class for two years. I also had visiting privileges for the hospital—they gave me an ID card and a parking pass for my car but fate was not too far behind. Seven years ago, I had a third heart attack, and I was sent to Vancouver—it was my eightieth birthday. I celebrated it in the hospital and for my present, they gave me a triple bypass heart operation.

My wife had had two strokes by this time, and she was getting around using a walker. She fell and broke her hip and was operated on but never walked again. I took care of her for as long as I could but finally it was too much and they had to put her in a nursing home, where she has been for the past four years. This made me scale back my ministry, as I go every day to visit her. I am very fortunate the nursing home is only one kilometer from where I live

CHAPTER 22

BUILDING A CHURCH

At this point, I would like to digress. We had a charismatic Catholic group come into the Rock Creek area, who attended our church. They made it a commune, with people coming and going, and I got along with them quite well, as I was still pastor of our congregation. But the church was in Bridesville, at the extreme west end of our church congregation. To be more central, we got the use of an empty Anglican church three miles east of Rock Creek. All we had to do was to keep the church up, pay the light and oil bills, and we could have our Sunday evening services there.

Soon, we were talking about building our own church in Rock Creek, which was more central; twelve miles to the west was Bridesville, eleven miles to the north was Westbridge, and eleven miles east was Midway. So, we started to look around for a suitable piece of property. Because I had not taken any money for ministering, we had a sizable amount in the building fund.

There was a new subdivision, divided into three-acre lots, just north of Rock Creek on the edge of town, beside Highway 33 North, to Kelowna. Each lot was $10,000, and after we bought one lot, the building program started. In one year's time, we were able to move into the lower auditorium. The main floor was still only a shell and we paid as we went along.

Kettle River Chapel

We experienced miracles during the building of our church. The men of the congregation were mostly employed by the Pope and Talbot sawmill at Midway. The mill had shipped out a carload of lumber to a customer, who rejected it and sent it back, so they had to have a quick sale of the lumber. One of our church members was authorized to buy it for one thousand dollars. It was one inch by eight inches, shiplap lumber and finished on one side, so we had lumber for the subfloor, and sheeting for the whole outside of the church, and for the inside ceiling.

For lining all the inside walls and the Sunday school rooms, we used gyproc. The church was not a small building. On one side of the lower auditorium we had a furnace room, a kitchen, and three Sunday school rooms and then on the opposite side, we had room enough for

I Am My Brother's Keeper

ten tables with folding legs. There were two doors to go out and several windows in between. Because we were on the ground level, the other three sides were in the side of the bank.

When a new church is planned, or a major renovation is needed, our district headquarters sends out a "Minute Men" appeal. Each man or woman who joins this group is approached by letter to give a small amount from two to five dollars, no more than three times a year. So you see, it doesn't put much strain on any one person.

When we built our church, the Minute Men donations added up to over eleven thousand dollars, so we had some cash to start with. This paid for our dimensional lumber, the roofing, the ready-mix concrete for the basement, and for the outside siding.

We had a lot of volunteer help. One man levelled off the ground for the front of the church parking lot. Then we had a bit of an upgrade and levelled off a large area for a second parking lot. Alf J. was a builder, who spent all of his time working in building churches for the Lord in India and other foreign fields. He agreed to come to Rock Creek and help us get started on our church and he stayed at our home. I had a subdivision in Rock Creek and was busy finishing off the house I was building, so I didn't do too much to help build the church. The Midway sawmill was shut down, however, so we had plenty of labour from men who worked at the mill.

We had the basement in and the walls framed when the men were called back to work at the mill. By then, I had my house finished and that set me free to spend more time helping to build the church. Alf J. wanted to leave for some reason or another and now that the church had its walls up, the church members asked me to take over, which I did. Some of the men who didn't live too far away would come and give a hand. Several of the men who had to go by the church, left home early so that they could stop and help out for a few hours before going on to work the afternoon shift.

When it was time to put on the roof, we had the trusses delivered from Penticton. As the church was forty feet wide and sixty feet long, this was no easy task but it was done and a smaller sawmill donated enough lumber to sheet the roof. Several of the men helped nail down the shingles, and we had our church shell built. In Kelowna, there was a business called the Auction Dome, and every Wednesday they held an auction sale, where anything and everything was sold.

I had eight rental units at that time and had furnished them all from the auction sale, so I was there quite often. The first thing I bought for the church was a set of doors for the main entrance. They were brown in colour, which was just right, and were made of solid hardwood with a large brass handle on each door. When we had them installed in the church, the building inspector, whom I had gotten to know quite well, said that you couldn't buy those handles for less than fifty dollars apiece. At the auction, I had bid ten dollars, and with no one bidding against me, I ended up taking them home. All of the windows for upstairs and downstairs were still in their crates and I was able to get them for a fraction of the price. I did all the wiring in the church, and we decided to heat the basement with electric heaters.

The auction had a large, dome-shaped building with rows of seats, a coffee bar, and offices where you went to pay for your purchases. All the good, more expensive merchandise was on the stage in front. The auction was never over before midnight. There was a big shed right, next to the dome, which was so full of things there was no room for benches. Outside in the yard, bigger things were sold, like cars, for example. The selling started at the outside at 6:30 p.m., and when everything was sold, they went inside the shed, and then into the dome.

I arrived a little late and they were selling outside in the yard but I ran inside the shed and there, against the wall, was a pile of electric heaters of all sizes—just what I needed. A man came over to me as I was checking them out and I said, more to myself than to him, that I wondered if half of them were burned out. "No," he said, "they are mine, I brought them." He told me that they had been used for only one season, because when the gas line came by his house, he changed over to gas and took the electric heaters out.

They were as good as new. I placed my hand on them and I claimed them in Jesus' name for our church. As they were sold in one lot, I bought the whole bunch for $140. These heaters would normally sell for about $1000. We had three 3000-watt heaters in the basement, a 1000- watt heater in each Sunday school room, a 1500-watt heater in the kitchen, and a 500-watt heater in each bathroom, with heaters left over.

One of our members, Royce S., was quite a handyman; he had his own shop with all the tools needed to build our heating system for upstairs. He had plans to make up a wood-burning furnace with two forty-five gallon drums; one on top of the other, with pipes to carry the heat to the other end of the church and an air return box. Then, we had a large fan and electric motor to move the heat to the front. It worked quite well, and the fire marshal passed it. We had lots of firewood, so the heating bill was quite low. I did all the plumbing but we needed to have a well drilled.

The young people dug a water line from the well to the church and I installed the pump. Next, we needed a septic tank and again, the young people dug the hole. The tank had to be six feet wide and ten feet long (outside measurements). I framed it and we mixed the cement and poured it. Then we needed one hundred and fifty feet of drain tile down thirty inches, which the young people dug. (My daughter, Sharon, her husband, Glenn, and Richard, the young pastor, had a Young People's group, which would have been the envy of larger churches.)

Next, was the job of dry-walling and taping. The sheets, standing on their edge, were four feet wide and ten feet long, so we needed more manpower than just the two of us. But after we had the church boarded-up, Richard and I did the taping and we involved the women by getting them to do the painting.

We built the kitchen cabinets and ten tables with folding legs, so we could accommodate about one hundred people at a banquet. Richard went with me to pick up the pale-yellow aluminum siding, some emergency lights, and crash bars for the doors. We made an agreement that we would not use the church as a sob story in order to get cheaper prices. This was not the way to do proper business as Christians. Everything we bought (kitchen counters for the cupboards, electrical supplies, and all of the siding) was sold to us at the contract price. All we had to do, when they made up our order, was to tell them it was for the Kettle River Chapel.

One day, while I was working alone taping gyproc, it was time to call it a day. I had a five-gallon plastic pail, about two-thirds full of soft mud. Coming down the stairs, my heel caught the steps and I lost my balance. The pail of mud got ahead of me and I landed at the bottom of the cement floor. I fell on the pail, which was lucky. The pail was flattened, the mud went out onto the cement floor, and my head went into the mud. One of the lenses from my glasses was missing, and I had quite a gash between my eyes.

I got to the medical clinic just as the doctor was leaving. He took me back into the office and sewed up my wound. I didn't have a headache or experience any pain, and when I went back to get the stitches out, the doctor was so amazed. He grabbed me and took me to a big mirror on the wall. He was amazed at how nicely the wound had healed; when he was sewing it up, he had said that I would probably have to have some plastic surgery to fix the scar. Today, you can't even see a scar. As I am writing this account of building the church, I realize that all of the jobs I've had and all of the trades I've learned were God preparing me to build this church.

The church was not the "Church of the Wildwood," that we had heard sung about, but this was the "Church on the Hill." Our driveway was a little steep but the church at the end of the driveway stood out nice and plain for all to see. It stood there as a welcome monument and a real credit to a small village called Rock Creek. It was the only decent building to have weddings and funerals and family gatherings in and for the dedication of children to the Lord.

We welcomed anyone who wanted to use it for legitimate reasons. Once, we had a party that had a wedding and then wanted to follow up with a dance. I told them we had built a church, not a dance hall, and if they didn't carry out their boom boxes, I would carry them out for them. They left faster than they came in. We did not charge rental for the use of the church, only a few dollars to pay the janitor to clean up.

I Am My Brother's Keeper

CHAPTER 23

SAGEBRUSH LODGE

Sagebrush Lodge was built in Osoyoos in 1978. It was an intermediate care home and could accommodate fifty-five residents. The local ministers of the churches had their own churches and were not interested in taking on any extra responsibilities. A retired United Church minister from Rock Creek, who was a friend of mine, took it upon himself to drive to Osoyoos and give the seniors a Sunday morning service. But it got to be too much for him and he was relieved when I volunteered to take over. I was no longer pastor of our church in Rock Creek and we had finished the building project with only the carpet on the upper auditorium left to be done. We had a dedication of the church with two hundred and seven people in attendance.

Kettle River Chapel Church dedication

I had the privilege of cutting the ribbon and they gave me a nice large jackknife engraved with my name and the church name as a little token of their appreciation for being the building foreman. Being the joker that I am, I said, "So, this is all they think of me—just a 'jackknife carpenter.'" Well, they all had a good laugh over that. But, it was a gift that I really treasured. I stayed on at the church as a maintenance man and started the fire that heated the church every Sunday morning, until we left Rock Creek. My pianist, from when I ministered in Rock Creek, got a job at Sagebrush Lodge as a nurse in training. She wanted to see that the seniors had a regular Sunday morning service, so she asked the management if I could take over the Sunday morning service and said she would be willing to supply the singing and the music.

They agreed, and I was at Sagebrush Lodge for the next five and a half years. The summer months were fine, but as soon as it got cold, I would go to the church early and start the fire. By 9:30 a.m., the first man of the congregation would arrive to take over, and I would hurry

I Am My Brother's Keeper

home and dress, and drive to Osoyoos in time for the 11 a.m. service.

As the driveway to the church was a little steep, we had arrangements made with a man who had a snowplow to come plow the driveway early Sunday mornings when it had snowed on Saturday. We were next door to the Department of Highways and they had a large stockpile of sand, to which they gave us permission to help ourselves. So, I would get the fire going and then load up my pickup and sand the driveway.

I had an enjoyable ministry with the seniors at Sagebrush Lodge. I will relay one incident I had. An elderly lady came to the Lodge... or I think it would be more accurate if I said she was put there by her family. Now, being the friendly guy that I am, I walked up to her and said, "Jesus loves you, and I love you," not aware of the fact that she had a cane in her hand. She swung it at me and narrowly missed. Every Sunday morning, I made a special effort. Taking care to stay out of the striking zone, I told her that Jesus loved her and I loved her. One day, it got to be too much for her and she blurted out at me, "Why would you love an old crank like me?"

I answered, "Sweetheart, I know you are here against your wishes, and you're not happy here. There's nothing I can do to get you out of here but I can be your friend and that's what I would like to be."

She started to look forward to me coming and visiting her and I could put my arm around her and love her. She had been a specialized nurse in her profession and her situation was like many other cases. The children would commit them to the Lodge thinking, *Oh well, they are fed and cared for, what more do these old people need?* Then they feel free of their responsibility. Soon, more residents needed more care and were sent to Oliver, to the extended care unit. Having made friends with them in Sagebrush, I followed them to Oliver. I would hold our Sunday morning service then drive the twelve miles to Oliver to visit in the extended care unit. This unit was built onto the hospital, at the west end on a lower level. So, you could get on an elevator and go up and be in the hospital.

Soon, I was visiting patients in the hospital; I will elaborate on just a few of these. Linda S., my piano player, left Sagebrush to go on to higher learning, and Betty B., a gifted musician, asked if she could come to Sagebrush and play the piano for the services. She attended the United Church but would leave an hour before her service was over, to come and play the piano for me.

Her husband had died and she had married again. Her second husband, Norman, had a bad heart and soon he was spending as much time in the hospital as he did at home. He had also attended the United Church but because of some disagreement, he had stormed out of the church and vowed never to darken the door of another church. So, he was in and out of the hospital. I had met Betty and Norman at their home and used to visit him at the hospital. He was a likable man but when I went to visit him at the hospital after our Sunday service, Betty would always caution me not to talk religion to him—he had had it up to here, she told me, motioning to her neck. So, I didn't talk religion but I always stopped to visit him. Then I would cry, driving home after our visit, "Lord, he is dying and I can't talk to him about accepting You as his Savior."

One day, I came into his ward at the hospital and he was alone in his bed, half sitting up. As I walked in, he saw me, came off the bed, and walked towards me with his arms stretched out as if he was in a trance. I reached my arms out and folded them around him. My heart went out in such love and compassion to him and I said, "Norman, if I don't try to lead you to the Lord, I would be worse than a murderer. Won't you accept the Lord as your Saviour?" He did and was born again into God's kingdom. He found the peace and joy that he was missing.

I stopped in Osoyoos to tell Betty that Norman was now a Christian; he had accepted the Lord, and she was overjoyed. Once again, the Holy Spirit witnessed to me to trust Him; "All things work together to them that love the Lord." Not too many months later, Norman passed away. He had been in and out of the hospital. One day, a little earlier, I had a phone call from Betty, who was at the hospital with Norman, and she said that he was dying. We were fifty miles from the hospital and I said to give me an hour and I would be there. An hour later, I walked into Norman's room. He was in a comatose state, but I said, "Norman, this is Leonard. Do you still love the Lord?" A big smile came over his face but Betty, standing behind me, didn't see him smile. She said that he hadn't heard me but I knew that he had. At five o'clock the next morning, he passed away.

Betty had him cremated, then asked me to do his memorial service.

She had a big living room and only wanted the family and close friends to attend. Norman had one daughter who came and Betty's four children came—two boys and two girls. I had met the two girls and one of the boys earlier. The other boy had made the army his career and was a captain in the Provost Corps—the military police.

As it was quite private, I was able to share how I'd led Norman to the Lord. At the luncheon, the son who was in the army came to me and said it was sure nice of me to share so privately about Norman. The oldest girl, Lee, said to me that it was the nicest funeral service she had ever attended. While we were eating lunch, Betty came up to me with an envelope. I told her that I could not take money from her but she insisted and opened my suit pocket and put the envelope in. I forgot all about it until I was halfway home, so I reached into my pocket and took out the envelope. While driving I couldn't count it, but there were some large bills in it. I had met Betty's brother, Howard S.; he was one of our missionaries in St. Lucia. Howard had a friend in Abbotsford and had at one time given me the friend's address; he was the contact person for sending Bibles to the people in St. Lucia. I just wrote the address on the envelope and sent it. How many Bibles it bought I don't know—only the Lord knows.

It was a hot summer afternoon and I was at the Oliver hospital. I had taken Pete, a patient I'd been seeing, outside to sit in the shade; he had dementia quite bad. I took him back into the hospital, to his ward, and across the room was a man who was up in years (I later found out he was eighty-four). The man was half-sitting up in bed, the left side of his face was pulled down, and an oxygen tube was in his nose—the result of a very bad stroke. It felt like a magnet was drawing me to him. I walked up to his bed and said, "Well hello, old timer," and growling more than speaking, he said, "Don't talk to me. I'm going to commit suicide."

I didn't know how this would be possible but in that moment, such love and compassion came over me that I said, "No, no, no. You have to accept the Lord and then when you leave this world, you will go to Heaven." I was surprised that I had caught his attention so quickly, so I explained salvation to him. I said that I knew he didn't sleep well and he said that the nights were hell and that he couldn't sleep.

So, I told him, "Tonight, when you can't sleep, look up to Heaven and talk to Jesus, just like you are talking to me. Ask Him to forgive any sins. The Bible says in Romans 3:23, 'For all have sinned and fall short of the glory of God.' Ask Jesus to come into your heart and you'll be born again into the kingdom of God." I was surprised at how he paid attention to me. I told him that I'd come back tomorrow and see him. I didn't tell him that I had to go to Penticton the next day and that I would just stop and see him. His name was Ed. The next day, I walked into Ed's room and his face lit up. "You really did come back?" he asked. I said, "I told you I would." He said, "I did what you told me—I asked Jesus to forgive my sins and come into my life."

In that moment, I had an experience I had never had before. I saw in my spirit Ed's mother on her knees praying for him and before I realized what I was saying, I said, "Ed, your mother was a Christian," and he replied, "Yes, my mother was a fine Christian." I prayed for him and left. Four days later when I came to see him, he was rejoicing in his newborn faith but I came again a few days later and his bed was empty. I knew the head nurse at the hospital so I asked, "Where is Ed? His bed is empty." She said that he had died that morning at five o'clock, and that he went really peacefully, exactly eleven days after I had first met him.

I rejoiced, not so much in that I had led Ed to the Lord, but in the fact that I had been obedient to the leading of the Holy Spirit when I felt that tug of the Holy Spirit to go to Ed's bed and talk to him. The faithfulness of God is beyond measure. Ed's mother prayed all her life and died not seeing Ed saved. But God chose me to answer her prayers. This was the greatest thrill to me and I have no doubt that had I not been there, or had not been obedient to the leading of the Holy Spirit, God would've chosen someone else to speak to Ed. But Ed's mother's prayers would have been answered.

CHAPTER 24

HOLLAND LIBERATED

On May 10, 1940, without any warning, German troops marched into Holland and five days later, Holland surrendered and was under German occupation until liberation began in 1944; ending in May 1945. Because the Canadian troops played such a major role in the liberation of Holland, in 1984, marking forty years since Holland's liberation, the Kelowna Canadian Legion decided to have a celebration. Greenwood was central for the gathering of veterans coming from the north and the south Okanagan and from east and north of the Kootenays. The Greenwood Legion had a large brick building left over from the early mining days, which was suitable. They wanted a veteran minister to give the Padre address and I, Leonard Senft, was given the honour.

The Greenwood Legion building was at the west end of town, about a kilometer from the city park, where the ceremonies were to be held. We lined up at the Legion Hall and formed a parade to march down the main street. On both sides of the street, standing on the sidewalk, were the local people who came to watch us. There were some cars deployed for veterans who could not walk that distance—those with amputations and handicaps. They asked me if I wanted to ride but I said that I wanted to march with the troops.

There were several hundred veterans. We were a grand sight; the Legion members in their caps and blue jackets, wearing their medals. I was the only one walking on the outside in a brown suit, swinging my big black Bible. We marched into the city park, up to the band shell, and started the ceremony. The flags were lowered, two minutes of silence were observed, and the bugler played *The Last Post*. Then it was my turn to give the Padre address:

"As we are honouring Holland, it would be fitting to say something about Holland, and a little research soon reveals some very interesting things. The people of Holland were a very industrious people, building miles and miles of dikes, and the reclaimed land became the most fertile land in the entire world. They grew flowers and shipped hundreds of tons of bulbs around the world. They were noted for their dairy products; cheeses, sent out to many parts of the world, were produced from the milk of their Holstein cows. They had the largest diamond cutting factories in the world. Rotterdam and Amsterdam were also seaports.

"In the early seventeenth century, Holland had the largest merchant fleet in the world. The Dutch were seafaring people and had colonies in the East Indies and Dutch Guyana. In September 1944, the liberation of Holland began, and on May 4, 1945, Germany surrendered. The hardships the people of Holland suffered were hard to comprehend; the food rations were barely enough to keep them alive, they had no fuel for heat or lights, and every able-bodied man had been taken to Germany to work in the war factories. But the worst was yet to come. When the liberation started, the Germans destroyed miles and miles of dikes, which the people had so painstakingly built over the years. The dikes were broken down, allowing the North Sea to flood many villages and drown thousands of people, thereby slowing the advance of the allied troops. The army troops were wading in mud up to their knees.

"Liberty came on May 4, 1945, with the complete surrender of Colonel General Johan von Bloskowitz to Lieutenant General Charles Floulkes. Today, we feel so honoured to have been part of the liberation of Holland from the formidable enemy, the German Wehrmacht, and we pay the highest tribute possible to the people of Holland, who paid so high a price in personal suffering and privation to maintain their freedom.

"It is hard to say but true—we have an enemy who is out to destroy us and he is called the devil. This was caused by one man's disobedience (Adam). 'For as by one man's disobedience many were made sinners, so by the obedience of one man, many will be made righteous.' - Romans 5:19. 'For all have sinned and fall short of the glory of God.' Romans 3:23. And that means me as well as you. It does not mean that we are vile sinners, thieves, and murderers. We meet and live with people who live the highest standards in life, in a moral lifestyle, but it does not alter the fact that we were born with a sinful nature. We are accountable for our sin and one day we will all have to stand before God in judgement.

"God, in His mercy and love, has made arrangements to take care of our sins. 'For God so loved the world that he gave his only begotten son that whosoever believes in Him should not perish but have everlasting life.' John 3:16. And 1 John 1:8 says that, 'If we confess our sins, He is faithful and just, to forgive us our sins and to cleanse us from all unrighteousness.'

"God has made us freewill agents; we have the ability whether or not to choose to accept Jesus Christ as the one who died on the cross at Calvary in our place; our sacrificial lamb. As we accept Him as our Saviour and Lord, we are born again into the family of God and He becomes our Heavenly father. To reject so great a salvation is to pay the consequences of death. Romans 6:23 says, 'The wages of sin is death but the gift of God is eternal life through Christ Jesus our Lord.' Please make the right choice!"

CHAPTER 25

SHORT TESTIMONIES

Boys' Club

While I was a pastor in Rock Creek, we enjoyed some winter sports as well as summer sports and picnics. We had some great hills to slide down with toboggans and we had snowmobiles to ride. Then we would build a fire and have hot chocolate and lunch. One winter, I had a boys' club—thirteen boys aged twelve and thirteen. We built some go-carts and, come spring, we had a grand day racing them. One of our local church members had a large basement that we could use, so we had half an hour of devotions then we worked on building our go-carts. We got the plans from an *Illustrated Mechanics* book we had. One of our church members cut out the pieces in his shop with power tools. The carts all needed four wheels and each had to be built sturdy enough not to collapse when a boy sat in it.

One day, I went to Penticton to a lawnmower shop and bought as many loose wheels as it had. The boys also found some broken lawnmowers to rob the wheels from—we needed forty-eight wheels for a dozen go-carts. All winter, we sanded and painted and put the go-carts together, and for safety's sake, each one of the go-carts had to have an approved braking system. When all was ready, the question arose as to where we could race them. Johnson Creek Canyon was halfway between Bridesville and Rock Creek, with a bridge spanning the narrow top of the canyon. There was a sharp drop, and then it levelled off to quite a sizeable flat span at the bottom, where there was a good-sized government campground with tables, benches, fire pits, and toilets.

There was a bypass highway around the bridge, which was just the right grade to run our go-carts down, then the highway climbed up a ways, levelled off, and met the main highway half a mile up the road. I understood that we would probably not get permission to use the bypass, but I knew the road foreman quite well, and on the day we had our races, the road would not be busy because it was too early in the year for tourists. I stationed one man and his pickup at each end, just in case someone came down the road. That way, they could be stopped to prevent any accidents.

So we had our races. The pickups hauled the go-carts up the hill but they didn't need us to push them to come down. After the races, we handed out small prizes. There had been only one RV that wanted to come down to the camp, and he was a good sport and enjoyed watching the boys racing their carts. We made a fire; roasted some wieners and marshmallows, and the ladies brought lunch and a large container of lemonade to drink. Two ladies brought accordions and we sang choruses. The turnout was great; we had over one hundred people there. Each boy had brought his relatives to see him race; uncles, aunts, grandmas, and grandpas.

I told the road foreman what we had done and he suggested that we use a road down to the gravel pit below. That would've been great but no go-cart with small wheels would ever run on the gravel road. But all is well that ends well. Everyone had a good time and talked about the experience for a long time, and none of us were thrown in jail.

Hundred Dollar Bills

One day, while driving my mail truck, I was daydreaming and what was going through my mind was that if I had more money I would give it to the Bible Society. Then I listed some more names of organizations that I would like to help. All of a sudden, I saw a shower of one-hundred dollar bills floating in my vision through the windshield. By the time I

I was visiting with Karl and Hazel and as usual, she made a pot of tea and served some cakes. When we were finished, Karl said, "Maybe you could explain to us the salvation you preach." This was the opening that I had been waiting for so I explained salvation to them; that they could be saved right now. I had them hold hands and as I was sitting in the middle, I placed my hands on top of theirs and led them in a sinner's prayer. Two more souls were won for the Lord.

I never get over how the Holy Spirit can save when we stay out of the way. Time passed, and Karl and Hazel both enjoyed being part of our congregation and coming to all our social functions. Karl died and I had the honour of performing his funeral service. They had two plots in Bridesville Cemetery. Hazel had relatives in Prince George and left us to go to live near them. A few years passed and we left Rock Creek, moving first to Osoyoos for three years, then to Kelowna. While there one day, I got a phone call that Hazel had passed on and that the body would be brought to Bridesville, to be laid next to her husband. Hazel had requested that I do the committal service.

My wife and I went to Bridesville and I did the committal service. Afterwards, the ladies had a delicious lunch prepared in the Bridesville Hall. Rosie and I left to go home, knowing this was not the end but that one day, we would all meet again in Heaven.

Brian P.

Hebrews 7:25: "Therefore He is also able to save to the uttermost those who come to God through Him, since He always lives to make intercession for them."

Sutherland Hills is a large nursing home in Kelowna and since I was not a pastor of a church anymore, I had a lot of free time. So they asked me if I would fill in when their regular pastor was away. I went on Sunday afternoon and Wednesday morning, whenever they would call me. One Sunday, I went to our Sunday morning service and Sutherland Hills called me to do an afternoon service, which I did. Then I went to the hospital to the rehab section to do visitation.

It was their supper hour at the rehab. I was tired and my car was not far from the entrance to the rehab section. All of a sudden, I got a

I Am My Brother's Keeper

strong urge to go to the cafeteria and have a coffee first. It didn't make sense—I had to go all the way back to the main entrance of the hospital where the coffee bar was—but tired as I was, I walked back and got in line. There were several people in front of me when one young man in hospital blue pyjamas stepped in front of me and kept looking at the lapel of my suit. I was wondering what he was up to when he looked up at me and asked if I was a minister. I said yes, realizing what he had been doing—he was trying to read my ID card. It was at that point that he said that he needed help. I asked him for his name and room number. He told me and ran out the door. His name was Brian.

The cashier lady remarked that he hadn't paid for his coffee. By then, I was in front of her and she said she had overheard our conversation. She was a volunteer who was up in years, a motherly looking type, and she had overhead him asking for help. She suggested that I had better go visit him. He had overdosed with drugs and they had brought him in yesterday and pumped out his stomach. I sat down, slowly drinking my coffee and wondering what this was all going to lead to. I went to the information desk to ask directions, and the man in charge said, "You can't go in there—that is the psych ward." Then when he saw my ID, he changed his mind, pointing me towards the elevator that would go up to that ward. I walked into the young man's room but it was empty. As I turned to leave, he came running into the room.

I sat him down crossways on the bed and pulled up a chair in front of him. I took each one of his hands in mine and looked him straight in the eye. "Brian, start talking. You want help and I want to know what the problem is." So, he started to talk. As a teenager he'd gotten into drugs but he got converted and attended the Presbyterian Church. He was now thirty-three years old and had been clean of drugs for quite a few years. Then he said, "I don't know what possessed me but I took a drug and I was right back to the addiction. And sooner than try to lick the habit, I tried to overdose to get it over with."

I told him, "You know what you have to do. You have to ask for the Lord's forgiveness, then do your part to stay clean." I prayed with him and asked the Lord to come back into his life.

Just before I left, he gave me a big hug, declaring, "Now we are brothers, aren't we?" Then he asked if I could get him a King James Version Bible. I came back a couple of days later and gave him a Bible and he had the joy of the Lord. I visited him a few times more and then he told me that they were sending him to a halfway house. I don't remember the name of the house.

We went to Saskatchewan soon after, and I never saw him again. I pray that he will stay clean and I will meet him again in Heaven. Next time I feel a great urge for a cup of coffee, I will be a little quicker to obey.

A Flat Tire

Hebrews 13:2: "Be not forgetful to entertain strangers for thereby some have entertained angels unawares."

We were driving to Osoyoos one day in a three-quarter ton pickup, which had truck-sized tires. Out of Rock Creek about six miles west, you go over a bridge, which spans Johnson Creek. It is not a long bridge but you drive down a slight incline, then on the other end is a little steeper incline, and to the left there is quite a curve in the road. We had driven over the bridge and were halfway around the curve when, "bang!" a back tire blew. I said to Rosie that my back was so sore I couldn't change that tire. (Backaches seem to be my constant companion but this day it was really bad—I could hardly climb into the truck.)

Right behind us appeared an older truck driven by a young man. He pulled ahead of us and stopped, then came over to our truck and asked what the problem was. I told him that we had blown a tire, and that my back was so sore, I couldn't possibly change it. He asked where my jack and wheel wrench were and after I told him, he started to change the tire. He was just a young man; no hat on, a mop of dark-blonde hair, and he was whistling the whole time (a tune I didn't recognize). In no time flat, he had the tire off, had thrown it into the back of the pickup, and had the spare tire mounted.

I offered to pay him something for the job, but he said, "No, thank you," kept whistling, and got in his truck and drove off. I was just so thankful, I was praising the Lord, then I realized when we got to the top of the grade and looked ahead, the young man was nowhere in sight. Hebrews 13:5 says, "I will never leave you nor forsake you," and Matthew 28:20 reads, "And lo I am with you always, even unto the end of the world." This must mean that the Lord is with us even when we have a flat tire and are unable to change it ourselves.

A Close Call

One winter day, while I was driving my mail truck, I saw an out-of-control car coming down a long, sloping hill that was quite icy. I knew that he would hit me so I crowded over as far as I could to the right side of the road. He was sliding sideways and there was about twenty feet before he would hit me. There was a patch of sand across the road. The sanding truck must have stopped long enough to allow the sander to build up a patch of sand.

When the car hit that sand, his wheels were just spinning like a buzz saw. The sand caught the car and shot it over the bank like a slingshot. The bank was quite steep and he cleared the shoulder of the road then plunked down into about two and a half feet of snow. All I could see was the taillights of the car. When I went over to see what had happened and if the driver was hurt, he was coming out of the car. He was not hurt but he was praying to the wrong god. He was just swearing and cursing God. He was a middle-aged salesman and I told him that he had better thank God that he wasn't hurt and not curse Him. God was again faithful to keep His preacher alive.

Helen J.

John 3:3: "Jesus answered and said unto him, 'Verily, verily, I say unto you, except a man be born again he cannot see the kingdom of God.'"

The last eight years that I drove the mail truck, my route was redirected to go from Rock Creek to Bridesville and Osoyoos. I had sold my freight license (H plate) and had given up the Coca-Cola agency. The children were growing up and leaving home. So I did not need to earn so much money and I would have more time to minister. I would arrive in Osoyoos at 10:30 a.m. then have to wait for half an hour more for the mail to be sorted for me to take back.

To kill the time, I often went to Mr. Mike's Café, where a group of pensioners—women and men—would meet for a morning coffee break. This was quite interesting, as everyone had stories to tell and experiences to share. I met Helen at the coffee break. Her husband had died years ago and she had her own mobile home. A man had moved in to share the home with her but he never came to our coffee breaks. After several years, I got to know her quite well. Then she was gone and I didn't see her for a few years.

One day, while I was visiting at the Oliver hospital, there came Helen down the hall in a wheelchair. She was overjoyed to meet up with me again. She had deteriorated quite quickly and had been placed in the extended care ward, which was attached to the hospital on the west side, one level lower. I started to visit her on a regular basis, led her to accept Jesus Christ as her saviour, and she was born into God's divine family. When I came to visit her, the first thing she would say was, "Len, pray for me. I always feel so good when you pray for me."

When we moved to Kelowna it wasn't as easy to go visit Helen, so when I was driving through Oliver, I decided to pay her a visit. I asked a nurse where her ward was and she said, "Helen is too far gone. She won't recognize you, but I will take you to her bed."

When we walked in, I said, "Hello, Helen," and she answered, "Hello, Len." Here is another one that I will meet again in Gloryland.

Osoyoos Lions Club

In 1994, we left Rock Creek and moved to Osoyoos, where we lived for three and a half years. I was just recuperating from a second heart attack. My mail contract had been cancelled, but we had eight rental units by then and since I had had the heart attack, I knew I would have to leave. The rental units needed constant attention to monitor them.

I would never turn anyone away if they needed a place to live. I never took a month's rent in advance, so consequently, a lot of renters would vacate the units leaving me with a month or two of unpaid rent and in some cases a lot more in arrears. But I always wanted to have my Christian testimony come first. There was also snow to shovel, so we decided to sell out and we moved to Osoyoos.

The Lions Club had been quite active in Osoyoos but in time had fallen apart. Now Bill C., who owned the Osoyoos book supply store, asked me if I would be interested in getting the Lions Club started again. I said I would. He didn't know why I was interested in the Lions Club.

Jenine, my niece in Victoria, was thirteen years old and had been riding a horse at her friend's place. When the horse stepped in a hole and tripped, Jenine went sailing over his head and hit the ground, breaking her neck in two places. Her recovery was a long story but the Lions Club came on the scene. They built a cement ramp from the sidewalk to the house and widened the doors for the wheelchair. Then they put in a lift from the main floor to the basement where my brother and his wife had made special living quarters for Jenine.

So, here was not only an opportunity to give back for the Lions Club's help but also there would be men and women to minister to. We soon had two dozen members and had two meetings a month; they were always dinner meetings. One of the Lions members owned quite a large café with a dining room, which he gave to the Lions for their meals and meetings. Every charitable organization wants to have a religious element, so they appointed me to be their chaplain. This, to me, was quite an honour. I was asked to say grace at all of our meetings and banquets, and sometimes to make the presentation of a gift for a special speaker that was invited.

When we left Osoyoos and moved to Kelowna, the club presented me with a nice wall plaque. It is oval in shape, about eight by eleven inches with a gold-coloured frame enclosing the Lions Club logo and a metal plate in the middle with my name engraved on it. This is a memento that I will always cherish. My ministry was only three years with the club, but I have the assurance that I left a lasting impression there. Only eternity will tell if we made lasting results.

Jimmy G.

In Osoyoos, they had a Choosing Wellness club for seniors, who gathered every Thursday morning at eleven a.m. until noon. We each donated one dollar, for which we received the following benefits. First, we were registered and received a card onto which, after we were weighed, our weight was recorded. Then, we had a nurse who took our blood pressure and recorded it onto the card. Then, several ladies were there to give massages, finishing off with a table of goodies—cookies, cakes, and drinks, tea, coffee, and juice, which made it an enjoyable morning.

In the winter months, we had a lot of extra people (snowbirds) who would come from the prairies, rent a motel unit, and stay the winter months. It was always nice to welcome these people and make them feel they were amongst friends; they were always seniors. They'd leave in the spring to go back home. Being a pastor, I was not specifically appointed but I was kind of expected to make contact with the new people who were coming in. One day, Jimmy came to the group. He was not a Snowbird; he and his wife had bought their own home in Osoyoos.

Jimmy came into our group one Thursday morning. Since he was a stranger, I welcomed him into the group. He was a senior, a few years older than I was, and was already showing signs of dementia. He took to me and I liked him right off the bat. So, when I asked him to join our Lions Club, he was more than willing.

Sometimes, I was asked to go to Penticton to some function, or to hear a special speaker at the Penticton Lions Club. On one occasion, they invited a blind lady and her Seeing Eye dog, which was very interesting as she showed us how they operated together. Jimmy was always ready and willing to go with me, and needless to say, we became good friends. He was short and stocky and had been a wrestler in his youth. He had old newspaper clippings of himself and the championships he had won. Jimmy went downhill quite fast, so they had to place him in Sunnybank nursing home in Oliver. I went to visit him as often as I could. While in Sunnybank, he met a lady who had lived in Saskatchewan, close to where I had grown up. She had read the book I had earlier written; *Pass the Potatoes Please,* and was quite pleased to meet me. Isn't it a small world?

I soon led her to the Lord and she was so happy to become a Christian. As I prayed for her when I visited her, she used to cry, not for sorrow but for joy. I had also led Jimmy to the Lord. Our move from Osoyoos to Kelowna was really hard on Jimmy; he couldn't understand why I didn't come to visit him any more. He and the lady from

I Am My Brother's Keeper

shovels back in, and His shovel is bigger than mine." God's laws are that we give first and then He gives back. I have been in ministry in one area or another until four years ago when I had to place my wife into a nursing home. As I go every day to visit her, I do not have much time to do anything else. To the best of my ability, I have fulfilled my father's wish for me to be a minister of the gospel and I have written this book, desiring that it will continue in ministry for the Lord. When we line up to receive our rewards (2 Corinthians 5:10: "We must all appear before the judgement seat of Christ, that each one may receive the things done in the body according to that he has done, whether it be good or bad."), I pray that on that day, my father will stand beside me to receive half of the rewards, for his prayers to dedicate me to preach the gospel and his many prayers while I was out preaching it. My father lived to be eighty-nine and was very proud of me when he heard me preach. What a satisfaction he must have felt that God had answered his prayers.

My success was no longer measured in the number of cows, pigs, and tractors I owned, but in souls won for the Lord and hearts mended. This world and all that is in it, its wealth and kingdoms, will pass away—only what's done for Christ will last. But first you have to know Him. As I close this book and say goodbye, I trust that if you have not already accepted the Lord Jesus Christ as your personal saviour, you will give some serious thought to this simple and easy salvation plan. Acts 2:21: "And it shall come to pass that whosoever shall call upon the name of the Lord shall be saved."

As a young man, I never missed an opportunity to better myself. As a *new man* in Christ, I have never missed an opportunity to be of service to someone and to lend a helping hand, for the glory of Christ Jesus and the joy of winning souls for Him. *I am my brother's keeper.* Amen.